SANCTIFICATION

SANCTIFICATION

CONSECRATION AND PURIFICATION

LESLIE M. JOHN

SANCTIFICATION

SANCTIFICATION

CONSECRATION AND PURIFICATION

LESLIE M. JOHN

My mission is to proclaim the good news of our Lord Jesus Christ as revealed to me through Holy Bible and from various teachers, preachers, and commentators. This is my voluntary service to God in the name of His only begotten Son Lord Jesus Christ. I share the truth of knowledge of God with others with good intention of bringing them to the knowledge of the living God, the God of Abraham, the God of Isaac, the God of Jacob, and the Father of our Lord Jesus Christ. My mission is to proclaim the Gospel of Lord Jesus Christ and not to convert anyone forcibly to Christianity. One may accept or reject any or part of my writings/teachings. No offense is meant to any individual or any religion or any organization.

Description:

This book brings out the truths about the Sanctification, which is whole-life time process. It can be divided into three phases:

1. Positional Sanctification
2. Progressive Sanctification and
3. Perfect Sanctification

ISBN-10:0989905853

ISBN-13:978-0-9899058-5-5

SANCTIFICATION

Contents

SANCTIFICATION

SANCTIFICATION

SANCTIFICATION

SANCTIFICATION

INTRODUCTION

It is such a refreshing and pleasant feeling after a shower. Unpleasant odor is washed away by the fresh water, and we are ready to go ahead with daily routine work. If we just let this little sweat stay on the body, it stinks after a while. It is true that if we do not wash our bodies for a day, it smells bad, and it can even lead to disease.

It would have been good if the freshness were to last for more than a day, but it does not. The simple reason is that our bodies are made of dust, and they return to dust when we die. God made it so, and no man can change it. Many a time when a full shower is taken in the morning subsequent shower is not necessary, for some, until evening, for some others, until next morning.

In the meantime, if the body sweats for some reason a full bath may not be needed but only a wash of that area where it sweats is enough. Sometimes even if we do not sweat, we wash our faces and eyes with water, to feel fresh.

King James Dictionary defines "Sanctification" as "The Act of Making a Thing Pure and Holy."

Reference: *For ye know what commandments we gave you by the Lord Jesus. For this is the will of God, even your sanctification that ye should abstain from fornication: That every one of you should know how to*

SANCTIFICATION

possess his vessel in sanctification and honour; (1 Thessalonians 4:2-4)

There are two aspects involved in Sanctification. Firstly, it is to set apart a man or animal as "holy." Secondly, to cleanse or to make pure man or animal. The sanctification is done for consecrating, that is to set apart as "holy" and keep man or animal, thus clean and pure.

After Pharaoh rejected, nine times, to let the children of Israel go from his presence the LORD God brought upon Egyptians the tenth plague by killing all their firstborn, of man and beast from Pharaoh's firstborn even to that of one in dungeon. In His great mercy towards His children, Israel, He spared all their firstborn; of man and of cattle.

The Lamb that was set apart on the tenth day was to be kept clean and on the fourteenth day it was offered as sacrifice to the LORD, and its blood applied to the doorposts, and the lintels of the homes of the children of Israel. The LORD passed over the houses of the children, where He saw the blood applied on the doorposts and lintels of their houses, and spared all their firstborn, while killing all the firstborn of Egyptians.

Lord Jesus Christ, who was the Lamb of God, offered Himself on the cross, as the firstborn of the Father, in order to redeem us from sin. Those who believe in Jesus will receive salvation.

Leslie M. John   *Page 14*

SANCTIFICATION

When the instructions were given to the children of Israel to set apart the Lamb that was to be slain the LORD claimed the firstborn as hallowed and said all the firstborn belong to Him. Every firstborn, of man and of cattle, was His and they were to be set apart as "holy" unto Him.

"Sanctify unto me all the firstborn, whatsoever opens the womb among the children of Israel, both of man and of beast: it is mine" (Exodus 13:2).

"That thou shalt set apart unto the LORD all that opens the matrix, and every firstling that cometh of a beast which thou hast; the males shall be the LORD'S" (Exodus 13:12).

The firstborn in every family is the property of the LORD God. It does not mean that the first born needs to be killed as a sacrifice, just as the Lamb was killed as sacrifice by the children of Israel, or set apart as a full evangelist, but it means that every firstborn male in every Christian family belongs to the Lord, and the firstborn should live for the Lord. Lord Jesus Christ died on the cross as the sacrificial Lamb on behalf of every sinner.

In the Old Testament period the Levite tribe was set apart as priests, instead of firstborn from other tribes, to serve the LORD in the Tabernacle.

"And I, behold, I have taken the Levites from among the children of Israel instead of all the firstborn that opens

Leslie M. John   Page 15

SANCTIFICATION

the matrix among the children of Israel: therefore, the Levites shall be mine" (Numbers 3:12)

Birthright is not to be taken lightly. Esau, the firstborn in Isaac's family gave up his birthright to Jacob for a meal and the result is seen even today. Esau's descendants are Edomites, and they are always at war with the children of Israel. Jacob, who was blessed and renamed as "Israel", was called by the LORD as His firstborn. Most blessings in Christian family belong to the firstborn.

God has recorded for our guidance that some of the firstborn, were not blessed because of their own doing. The first man, who was Adam's firstborn, Cain, was cursed because he killed his own younger brother, Abel. Seth, Adam's son, was blessed in his place. Jacob's firstborn was Reuben, but he was not blessed because he defiled his father's bed; in his place Judah was blessed.

On the night before Jesus was arrested, He knew that His hour has come that He should lay down His life bearing our sin upon Himself in order that whoever believes in Him shall receive salvation, He desired that should not miss participating in the Passover feast. He loved His disciples, and when supper was ended, the devil entered into the heart of one of His disciples, Judas Iscariot, who later betrayed Him.

EXEMPLARY SERVICE OF JESUS

Jesus rose from the supper, laid down his garments, took a towel and girded Himself. He was about to demonstrate an exemplary act which His disciples should learn and do as He did. He poured water into a basin, and began to wash the feet of His disciples, and wipe them dry with His towel.

When it was the turn of washing the feet of Peter, one of His disciples, Peter said to Jesus as to whether He would wash his feet! Jesus said to Peter that what He does would not be understood by him then, but later on he would know the meaning of washing his feet. Peter, as impulsive as he always was, replied to Jesus that He should never wash his feet.

Then, Jesus said to Peter that if He did not wash his feet he would not have any part with the Lord. Peter gives Jesus a surprising answer that He should wash not only his feet but his hands and head as well. Jesus said to Peter that he, who had a full bath does not need another bath, to clean a little of his body, but needs only a small wash of his feet. One reason Jesus said that 'Ye are clean, but not all' was because He knew Judas Iscariot was going to betray Him. Second reason could be that Peter was already washed fully and he does not need another full wash, but a little wash of his feet (cf. John 13:1-11)

"So after he had washed their feet, and had taken his garments, and was set down again, he said unto them, Know ye what I have done to you? Ye call me Master and Lord: and ye say well; for so I am. If I then, your Lord and Master, have washed your feet; ye also ought to wash one another's feet. For I have given you an example, that ye should do as I have done to you. Verily, verily, I say unto you, The servant is not greater than his lord; neither he that is sent greater than he that sent him". (John 13:12-16)

The example Lord Jesus Christ has set for us to follow is awesome. First of all, it teaches us that we, who are born-again, are secure in Him, yet because we are in the world, where we encounter innumerable temptations in our

SANCTIFICATION

daily life that it is possible that we fall from
the presence of the Lord.

The Ten Commandments given to the children
of Israel, during the time of Moses, were
condensed into two commandments by Jesus,
by saying that we should love the Lord our
God with all our heart, with all our soul, with
our mind, which is the first commandment and
the second one is to love our neighbors as
ourselves.

*"Jesus said unto him, Thou shalt love the Lord
thy God with all thy heart, and with all thy
soul, and with all thy mind. This is the first
and great commandment. And the second is
like unto it, Thou shalt love thy neighbour as
thyself. On these two commandments hang all
the law and the prophets". (Matthew 22:37-40)*

One may keep nine commandments out of Ten
Commandments but the 10th commandments
is, very hard, to keep. The Tenth
Commandment is:

*"Thou shalt not covet thy neighbour's house,
thou shalt not covet thy neighbour's wife, nor*

his manservant, nor his maidservant, nor his ox, nor his ass, nor any thing that is thy neighbour's" (Exodus 20:17)

The condensing of the Ten Commandments by Jesus into two, however, does not mean that He has abolished the Mosaic Law, but He came to fulfill the Law and set us on a higher plane and said:

"But I say unto you, That whosoever is angry with his brother without a cause shall be in danger of the judgment: and whosoever shall say to his brother, Raca, shall be in danger of the council: but whosoever shall say, Thou fool, shall be in danger of hell fire" (Matthew 5:22)

"But I say unto you, That whosoever looketh on a woman to lust after her hath committed adultery with her already in his heart".
(Matthew 5:28)

If so, then who can be saved? It appears none of us can be saved if we are to follow the law and keep it, but then, Jesus said, "... be of good cheer; I have overcome the world" (cf. John 16:33)

Apostle Paul said that there is no temptation that can over take our capacity to face it and be victorious over it. In addition God always will help us to overcome the temptation by providing escape route and God is faithful and never allows in a believer's life a greater temptation than that he could bear it. (cf. 1 Corinthians 10:13)

In spite of all such provisions, to keep one away from sinning, believer is likely to fall into sin. After all we are living in a wicked world and no one is perfect; and that is the reason why we need purification, cleansing. We need to be set apart to live a holy life. We need to be anointed with Holy Spirit to be triumphant over temptations. We need much grace from the Lord and cleansing of our sins every day in our lives. Except for grace through faith we cannot be justified. The Law points to the guilt and it does not give us salvation. It is only by grace from our Lord Jesus Christ that we can remain pure and sinless.

Leslie M. John   *Page 21*

SANCTIFICATION

Look not every man on his own things, but every man also on the things of others. Let this mind be in you, which was also in Christ Jesus: Who, being in the form of God, thought it not robbery to be equal with God: But made himself of no reputation, and took upon him the form of a servant, and was made in the likeness of men: And being found in fashion as a man, he humbled himself, and became obedient unto death, even the death of the cross. Wherefore God also hath highly exalted him, and given him a name which is above every name: That at the name of Jesus every knee should bow, of things in heaven, and things in earth, and things under the earth;
(Philippians 2:4-10)

CHAPTER 1
SANCTIFICATION: BIBLICAL DEFINITION

IN THE OLDTESTAMENT

Lexicon: Strong's H6942 – transliterated as "*qadash*"

Definitions: To consecrate, sanctify, prepare, dedicate, be hallowed, be holy, be sanctified, be separate, to be set apart, be consecrated, to be hallowed, and

IN THE NEW TESTAMENT

Lexicon: Strong's G38 – transliterated as "*hagiasmos*" *(noun)*

Definition:

1. consecration, purification
2. the effect of consecration

SANCTIFICATION

Sanctification of heart and life

Root word:

Lexicon: Strong's G37 – transliterated as
"hagiazō" (verb)

Definition:

- to render or acknowledge, or to be venerable or hallow
- to separate from profane things and dedicate to God
- consecrate things to God
- dedicate people to God
- to purify
- to cleanse externally
- to purify by expiation: free from the guilt of sin
- to purify internally by renewing of the soul

SANCTIFICATION

It is also apt to consider the method by which 'sanctification' is achieved.

Lexicon: Strong's G2758 -transliterated as "*kenoō (verb)*

Definition:

1. to empty, make empty
    1. of Christ, he laid aside equality with or the form of God
2. to make void
    1. deprive of force, render vain, useless, of no effect
3. to make void
    1. cause a thing to be seen to be empty, hollow, false

Root word:

Lexicon: Strong's G2756 *Kenos (Adj)*

Credits to: Study Resources: Dictionaries: Vines and Thayer's Greek Lexicon: Sanctification: Blue Letter Bible

SANCTIFICATION

CHAPTER 2
THE BASICS OF
SANCTIFICATION

Before we understand what 'sanctification' means we should understand the basic aspects of salvation, who the Lord Jesus Christ is, and why do we need to sanctify ourselves? It is essential that we have the knowledge of the truth about salvation; otherwise it becomes hard for us to understand why we need to consecrate to the Lord, and why we need purification of soul and conscience.

Way back in Exodus chapter 12 it is seen how the lamb was consecrated to become the sacrifice for the salvation of the children of Israel from the destruction that was about to come in fourteen days from the first day of the month of "Abib", a month denoted as such by the God of Israel. A pure lamb without any blemish was to be set apart on the tenth day of "Abib" and whole family would play with it and treat it as their family member.

SANCTIFICATION

*Speak ye unto all the congregation of Israel,
saying, In the tenth day of this month they
shall take to them every man a lamb,
according to the house of their fathers, a lamb
for an house: And if the household be too
little for the lamb, let him and his neighbour
next unto his house take it according to the
number of the souls; every man according to
his eating shall make your count for the lamb.
Your lamb shall be without blemish, a male of
the first year: ye shall take it out from the
sheep, or from the goats: And ye shall keep it
up until the fourteenth day of the same
month: and the whole assembly of the
congregation of Israel shall kill it in the
evening. (Exodus 12:3-6).*

On the night before 14th day of "Abib" which
was also called "Nisan" the lamb was killed and
its blood was applied to the doorposts and
lintels of the houses of the children of Israel in
order that their firstborn would not be killed
when the LORD passed over their homes.

PHYSICAL REDEMPTION

All the firstborn of Egyptians, including that of Pharaoh of Egypt, were killed by the LORD when He went in the midst of the land of Egypt that night. It was because of this serious plague that was brought on Egyptians and Pharaoh that they believed that God of Israel was powerful enough to redeem from the bondage of slavery under Pharaoh. It was then that the Pharaoh released the children of Israel from the bondage under him. Thus the children of Israel were saved from perishing.

However, as soon as the children of Israel left Egypt, Pharaoh chased them from behind with his chariots, horses and horsemen. Chariots, horses and horsemen were considered as the best weapons of war during those days; probably we could compare them with present day nuclear weapons. The children of Israel had nothing of that kind to protect themselves, but they had the strong and mighty arm of the LORD with them. The outstretched mighty arm of the LORD that delivered them from Egyptians was enough for them to defeat them.

The angel of the LORD who went before them removed Himself and went behind them.. When the Egyptians pursued the children of Israel from behind they saw darkness from the pillar of cloud that stood between them and the children of Israel. When the children of Israel looked back they saw in the light coming out from the pillar of cloud. Thus none of either party could approach one another. God's protection of His children was so strong that the enemy could not come near them.

Moses raised the rod over the Red Sea at the command of God, and the children of Israel passed the Red Sea on the dry ground in the midst of it when the waters on either side of their pathway stood like heaps until they, their children and their cattle safely passed over to the other side of the sea. When the Egyptians tried to break into the camp of Israel, the angel removed the wheels of the chariots of Pharaoh, and then all their chariots, horses, and horsemen drowned in the sea and were killed. Thus the children of Israel had their physical salvation, under the grace of God, while the might of the evil one perished.

And the angel of God, which went before the camp of Israel, removed and went behind them; and the pillar of the cloud went from before their face, and stood behind them: And it came between the camp of the Egyptians and the camp of Israel; and it was a cloud and darkness to them, but it gave light by night to these: so that the one came not near the other all the night. (Exodus 14:19-20)

God provided heavenly bread called "Manna" for them to eat and protected them throughout their journey through the wilderness for forty years. However, whenever the children of Israel committed abomination in the sight of the LORD by either worshipping other gods in the form of idols and/or committed whoredom, God chastised them heavily.

It was so sad that they committed wickedness repeatedly in the sight of the LORD and transgressed His commands. God chastised them over and over whenever they caused anger in the LORD's heart by committing wickedness in His sight. Every time they were chastised they returned to God crying in repentance because they would be unable to bear the chastisement and God forgave them. They again fall into sin, and when they are chastised they cry in repentance and God would forgive them, and they commit sin again. This was like a cycle in their lives, until God's anger burst against them when none of the generation that left from Egypt including Moses entered the Promised Land. Only the children born en-route their journey to Canaan, led by Joshua and Caleb entered the Promised Land.

If we were in that position, probably we would do greater wickedness than they did; who knows! Not that we are perfect, but these things happened the lives of Israel and recorded for our correction and reproof.

Most of the staunch followers of God committed sin in their lives, as we read in the

SANCTIFICATION

Old Testament, and they cried unto the LORD when they were chastised by Him. King David was a great example of falling into sin with Bathsheba and conspiring against her husband Uriah. However, he did not do such transgression as King Saul did in disobeying the LORD, but did what was right in the sight of the LORD, repented of his sin, and, therefore, he was restored. In fact, God knew in His foreknowledge that David shall fulfill all His will, and, therefore, God called him as "a man after mine own heart".

And when he had removed him, he raised up unto them David to be their king; to whom also he gave testimony, and said, I have found David the son of Jesse, a man after mine own heart, which shall fulfil all my will. (Acts 13:22)

CHAPTER 3
JESUS AND EARLY CHURCH

The writer of Hebrews quotes in part the prophecy of David as reiterated by Peter in Acts 2nd Chapter. The Father said to the Son that His throne is everlasting and a scepter of righteousness is the scepter of His kingdom. He said to the Son "Sit on my right hand, until I make thine enemies thy footstool"

Angels are ministering spirits that are sent forth to minister them that are heirs of salvation, and such salvation is by Lord Jesus Christ, the Son of God, alone. God spoke to the Children of Israel, as also to us by His Son, in the last days before latter's crucifixion that Jesus, His only begotten Son, was appointed heir of all things. The LORD spoke with the same power and authority that created the worlds.

Lord Jesus loved righteousness and hated iniquity, and therefore the Father, who is even His God, anointed Him with the oil of gladness

SANCTIFICATION

above His fellows. The Lord laid the foundations of the earth and the heavens, and they are the works of His hands. The worlds perish like garment, and the Lord will fold them up, and they shall change, but Jesus is same yesterday, today and tomorrow.

Apostle Paul writes about the relationship between the Father and the Son and our position. We give thanks to the Father, who gave us the privilege to be partakers of the inheritance of the same light. He delivered us from the power of darkness and translated us into the kingdom of his dear Son. We have redemption from our sin and forgiveness through the blood of Jesus Christ, "Who is the image of the invisible God, the firstborn of every creature"

"For by him were all things created, that are in heaven, and that are in earth, visible and invisible, whether they be thrones, or dominions, or principalities, or powers: all things were created by him, and for him: And he is before all things, and by him all things consist. And he is the head of the body, the

Leslie M. John   *Page 35*

*church: who is the beginning, the firstborn
from the dead; that in all things he might have
the preeminence" (Colossians 1:16–18)*

Jehovah exalted Him by His right hand and
ordered the angels of God to worship Him.
Peter says that the disciples are witnesses that
God raised His Son, Jesus from the dead. Jesus
appeared to them and many others, for forty
days, after His resurrection. Lord Jesus
received the promise, the Holy Spirit, from the
Father, and sent Him into this world, and by
His power they were able to witness the
miraculous speaking in various languages that
was understandable to every man who spoke a
different language. The communication was
made easy and they all could understand what
Peter spoke of the Gospel of Jesus Christ.
They all could speak to one another so easily
that even if they did not know any other man's
language everyone understood any other
man's language.

David spoke prophecy of Lord Jesus Christ,
who was going to be seated at the right hand
of the Father. The prophecy of David was

SANCTIFICATION

fulfilled when crucified Jesus, was buried, and rose from the dead, and ascended into heaven, and was seated at the right hand of the Father, as the writer of Hebrews reiterated about this fact.

Peter spoke to the house of Israel to be sure in their understanding that God made the Same Jesus, whom they crucified, both Lord and Christ. When the people heard the Gospel message from Peter, they were pricked in their hearts, and inquired him, and the rest of the apostles as to what they should do next.

Peter said to them to

"...Repent, and be baptized every one of you in the name of Jesus Christ for the remission of sins, and ye shall receive the gift of the Holy Ghost" Acts 2:38

In the same tone Peter continued saying the Promise is given to the children of Israel and to all that are far away as well, even as many as the Lord our God shall call. His message inferred that salvation is available not only Jews, but also to Gentiles. Peter gave

Leslie M. John   Page 37

testimony of Jesus with many other words and exhorted them to save themselves from the untoward and obstinate generation.

It was the first salvation message ever delivered on the face of the earth, after Lord Jesus ascended into heaven. Many believed Gospel message from Peter, and as many as believed in Lord Jesus Christ were baptized. The message had so great impact on the hearers that on the same day there were three thousand souls were added to them.

And then…

Peter and other disciples and all those who believed in Jesus "continued stedfastly in the apostles' doctrine and fellowship, and in breaking of bread, and in prayers" (cf. Acts 2:42)

"And they, continuing daily with one accord in the temple, and breaking bread from house to house, did eat their meat with gladness and singleness of heart, Praising God, and having favour with all the people. And the Lord added

SANCTIFICATION

to the church daily such as should be saved. Acts 2:46–47)

CHAPTER 4
ANGELS DESIRE TO LOOK INTO

Prophets spoke the future events by the inspiration from God, saying "thus says the LORD", not knowing what they spoke of concerning that which was to come much later. Prophecies are traced back from the New Testament assertions to connect to what was said in the Old Testament period. When such connection is made and seen it is evident that most of the prophecies, except that of eschatology, are fulfilled. There are many prophecies concerning the last days and the future, which are yet to be fulfilled. Except for Lord Jesus Christ, who was the Son of God, none of the prophets, who spoke prophecies knew what they were speaking; not even Daniel. The angel said to him to seal the prophecies and it is not for him to know but to those who are in the last days.

"But thou, O Daniel, shut up the words, and seal the book, even to the time of the end: many shall run to and fro, and knowledge shall

be increased. Then I Daniel looked, and, behold, there stood other two, the one on this side of the bank of the river, and the other on that side of the bank of the river. And one said to the man clothed in linen, which was upon the waters of the river, How long shall it be to the end of these wonders? And I heard the man clothed in linen, which was upon the waters of the river, when he held up his right hand and his left hand unto heaven, and sware by him that liveth for ever that it shall be for a time, times, and an half; and when he shall have accomplished to scatter the power of the holy people, all these things shall be finished. And I heard, but I understood not: then said I, O my Lord, what shall be the end of these things? And he said, Go thy way, Daniel: for the words are closed up and sealed till the time of the end" (Daniel 12:4–9).

Peter writing his first epistle, predominantly to dispersed Jews among Nations, infuses confidence in them and comforts them that they should rejoice in the Lord. Peter's address is applicable to Gentiles who received salvation based on 1 Peter 1:18, 2:10, 4:3

SANCTIFICATION

"Which in time past were not a people, but are now the people of God: which had not obtained mercy, but now have obtained mercy" (1 Peter 2:10).

Peter says that the trials and manifold temptations, which they were facing, were of short duration and their future is bright. The trial of their faith was much more precious than that of gold that perishes. A noticeable point is that Peter uses the word "Precious" several times in his epistles. We are redeemed by the precious blood of Lord Jesus Christ and our hope is precious. Obviously, he was addressing those who have already received salvation of their souls, and yet undergoing severe trials and temptations. God does not tempt us but surely He will test us. Even if our faith is tried with fire, it stands the test, and will be found more precious than that of gold, which perishes. Our firm stand for Christ in faith brings praise and glory to the Lord, even at His second coming. Addressing Gentiles, who have not seen Jesus, Peter says that they love Him and rejoice with unspeakable joy, full of glory to receive the reward of their faith, which is salvation of their souls. (cf. 1 Peter 6:9)

BY GRACE

The salvation by grace that Peter was explaining about was not known to Prophets, who, even without knowing what it was all about, diligently searched as to what it was.

Referring to His death and resurrection, when Jesus said, "Destroy this temple, and in three days i will raise it up", His disciples did not understand, but when he was risen, they remembered that he had said this to them beforehand, and then "they believed the scripture, and the word which Jesus had said". (cf. John 2:20–22)

The prophets prophesied of the grace that was to come to them and searched as to the time–phase such grace period would come. They did not speak for themselves, but they spoke for those who were there then and received preaching with the help of Holy Spirit. Even angels desired to know of that salvation by grace through faith would come about. (cf. 1 Peter 1:10–13)

"Of which salvation the prophets have enquired and searched diligently, who prophesied of the grace that should come unto you: Searching what, or what manner of time the Spirit of Christ which was in them did signify, when it testified beforehand the sufferings of Christ, and the glory that should follow. Unto whom it was revealed, that not unto themselves, but unto us they did minister the things, which are now reported unto you by them that have preached the gospel unto you with the Holy Ghost sent down from heaven; which things the angels desire to look into" (1 Peter 1:10–12).

CHAPTER 5
OF WHICH SALVATION?

Peter emphasized that the salvation by grace through faith was not understood by not only Old Testament Saints, but even the angels. The mystery of "One New Man" was hidden during the Old Testament period and it was revealed in the New Testament period.

That the Gentiles should be fellowheirs, and of the same body, and partakers of his promise in Christ by the gospel: (Ephesians 3:6)

Whoever believes Jesus as Savior, irrespective of whether he is a Jew or Gentile, or male or female, will receive salvation. The death of Jesus on the cross, His burial and His resurrection is to be acknowledged by the one who seeks salvation.

Having abolished in his flesh the enmity, even the law of commandments contained in ordinances; for to make in himself of twain

SANCTIFICATION

one new man, so making peace; (Ephesians 2:15)

That the Gentiles should be fellowheirs, and of the same body, and partakers of his promise in Christ by the gospel: (Ephesians 3:6)

Peter advises the dispersed Jews among Gentile nations, and Gentiles in those lands that they should gird up their loins of their minds, be vigilant, and hope to the end for the grace that was to be brought by Jesus at His second coming.

Peter quotes Old Testament verse (Leviticus 11:44), where the LORD God spoke to the children of Israel by the mouth of Moses and Aaron that they should sanctify themselves, and be holy because the LORD is holy. The LORD God commanded them through Moses that they should not defile themselves by eating any kind of food that was prohibited by Him.

Later Apostle Paul writes, by the revelation of Jesus Christ, not to allow anyone to judge them in meat, or in drink, or in respect of any holiday, or the new moon, or of the Sabbath days, and thus legalism is done away with. (Colossians 2:16)

Peter advises the dispersed Jews among Gentile nations, and the Gentiles in those lands that they should keep away from the kind of lusts that they lived in, before they became disciples of Jesus. He said that even in their conversations with others they were to remain holy because God called them holy. The spiritual man seeks spiritual things and fleshly man seeks fleshly pleasures.

While spiritual things bring blessings in one's life, fleshly things bring ruin. While gathering riches that are necessary for one's life is not sin, excessive gathering of riches out of greed, will bring ruin. Jesus said no man can serve two masters; either he will serve God or mammon (cf. Matthew 6:24, Matthew 19:24)

Every follower of Jesus Christ should know that the Father, whom they call on, is impartial in judging them of their work while they are on their journey to the eternal abode in heaven.

SANCTIFICATION

We are sojourners on this earth and our inheritance is in heaven.

Therefore, seek only the things that are needed in heaven and gather for future residence, the treasures that last eternally than that of the things that perish. We are redeemed from the bondage of sin not with corruptible things, such as silver and gold, or from vain conversations received by tradition from predecessors, but with the precious blood of Jesus Christ, who was the Lamb of God, without any blemish and without any spot.

Lord Jesus said:

Lay not up for yourselves treasures upon earth, where moth and rust doth corrupt, and where thieves break through and steal: (Matthew 6:19)

Lord Jesus Christ was chosen by the Father even before the foundation of the world that He should become the sacrificial Lamb of God, and accordingly He was on this earth and lived among us. He preached repentance, and the

SANCTIFICATION

imminent "kingdom of heaven". Jews rejected Jesus as their Messiah and, therefore, the establishment of literal kingdom was postponed, and the salvation was offered to the Gentiles as well. After the resurrection of Jesus from the dead, Apostle Peter, and other apostles, as also Apostle Paul, who followed them preached the Gospel of Grace, which was salvation by Grace through faith; and it was the gift of God.

Peter asserts that the disciples of Jesus and those from Gentiles, who were converted, do believe in God, who raised Jesus from the dead. They all believe that the Father gave back the glory to Jesus, who had it when He was with the Father. He had relinquished it, when He came into the world in the form of a servant, and in the likeness of man. When the glory of the Father was restored to the Son, He became the hope of all believers that they might have hope in Him. Peter's desire was that we all love one another fervently with a pure heart.

SANCTIFICATION

Those who believe in Jesus, and are born-
again are saved, not by corruptible seed, but
by incorruptible seed, by the word of God that
lives and abides in them for ever. The Lord
and His will endure forever, while the grass
withers and so do all flesh, and the entire
glory of man perishes as does the flower of
grass.

*Heaven and earth shall pass away, but my
words shall not pass away. (Matthew 24:35)*

*So shall my word be that goeth forth out of my
mouth: it shall not return unto me void, but it
shall accomplish that which I please, and it
shall prosper in the thing whereto I sent it
(Isaiah 55:11)*

Peter and other disciples as also Apostle Paul
preached this word of God. The word of God
does not perish nor shall pass away; but
endures for ever. The disciples preached the
Gospel of Jesus Christ, whose blood cleanses
us from all sin. Peter preached initially to Jews
and later to Gentiles as well, as we read in Acts

SANCTIFICATION

10; whereas Paul was chosen by the Lord to
preach primarily to the Gentiles (cf. Acts 9:15)

The Good News about the Gospel of Jesus
Christ is about His death, burial and
resurrection. He died on the cross, for our
sake and on behalf of us, bearing our sin upon
Him, in order that we may be delivered from
our sin, and that we may receive everlasting
life. The salvation is available for all those
who confess sins and accept Him as Savior,
and believes in heart that God raised Him from
the dead (Cf. Romans 10:9)

Old Testament saints prophesied about our
resurrection and had faith that they will see
God.

*"For I know that my redeemer liveth, and that
he shall stand at the latter day upon the earth"
Job 19:25*

(Cf. Psalm 6:5; Psalm 16:10; Psalm 17:15;
Psalm 30:3; Psalm 49:15; Psalm 73:24; Psalm
89:48)

SANCTIFICATION

Lord Jesus Christ, by rising from the grave showed us that we will not be left in the grave but rise from it to have everlasting life.

"But whosoever drinketh of the water that I shall give him shall never thirst; but the water that I shall give him shall be in him a well of water springing up into everlasting life" John 4:14

We are sealed with the Holy Spirit of Promise, and therefore, we should not grieve Holy Spirit by committing sins repeatedly.

"In whom ye also trusted, after that ye heard the word of truth, the gospel of your salvation: in whom also after that ye believed, ye were sealed with that holy Spirit of promise" Ephesians 1:13

"And grieve not the holy Spirit of God, whereby ye are sealed unto the day of redemption" Ephesians 4:30

Our salvation is secure and it will not be lost. Referring to those who are already saved by the precious blood of Jesus Christ, the Bible says that all of us were once enemies to God, and went astray like sheep, but then we are returned to the Shepherd by trusting Him as our shepherd. God loved us first and had compassion on us and He, who forgave us of our sins, is not human to backslide on His promise to take back the gift He gave us, but He chastises us when we go astray. It is by hearing that faith comes, and the hearing by the word of God. (cf. 1 Peter 2:25, Romans 10:17)

"But God commendeth his love toward us, in that, while we were yet sinners, Christ died for us". (Romans Ch. 5:8)

It is the Father in heaven, who sent His only begotten Son Jesus, draws men to come to Him, and Lord Jesus Christ, to whom all power is given by the Father, will raise from the dead, them that believed in Him (cf. John 6:44)

Ephesians chapter 2:8-10 reveals a great truth that the gift of salvation cannot be gained by doing any amount of good works, but it is received only by grace through faith in Jesus.

SANCTIFICATION

None can boast that he or she received salvation by doing good works; however, a true believer would live to do good works after he has received salvation by grace through faith. We are His workmanship, and therefore, He does not tolerate any sin. Every sin is abominable to God, and no believer, who commits sins after receiving salvation, would escape chastisement.

Christ is the head of the Church, and those that have Lord Jesus Christ as their personal savior, are the members of the Church. The Church is His bride and the bride is the possession of Lord Jesus Christ. When Lord Jesus Christ comes again the church is caught up to be with Him for ever and ever. He protects His treasured possession from the "great tribulation". Thus we are so privileged that our salvation is sealed with the Holy Spirit of promise, and no one can take away our salvation.

My Father, which gave them me, is greater than all; and no man is able to pluck them out of my Father's hand. (John 10:29)

SANCTIFICATION

Apostle Paul wrote:

In a moment, in the twinkling of an eye, at the last trump: for the trumpet shall sound, and the dead shall be raised incorruptible, and we shall be changed. For this corruptible must put on incorruption, and this mortal must put on immortality. So when this corruptible shall have put on incorruption, and this mortal shall have put on immortality, then shall be brought to pass the saying that is written, Death is swallowed up in victory. (1 Corinthians 15:52–54)

CHAPTER 6
SANCTIFICATION

GENERAL DEFINITION

Sanctification is setting apart, man or animal or a thing, for God. It is entering into relationship with Christ by faith.

DESCRIPTION

Know ye not that ye are the temple of God, and that the Spirit of God dwelleth in you? (1 Corinthians 3:16)

For New Testament believers, it is separation from evil ways and evil things. It is the will of God that in sanctification, believers should abstain from fornication. Believer's body is the temple of God and if anyone destroys the temple of God, He will destroy the temple. The body of believer needs to be preserved in sanctification as holy unto the Lord to His honor. The foremost requirement is abstaining from fornication, because God did not call us to become 'unclean' but to be 'clean' and 'holy'. (cf. 1 Thessalonians 4:7, 1 Thessalonians 4:3)

Just as Jesus emptied himself to not use his divine nature and became fully human we are to empty ourselves to not depend on our of strengths but do what Jesus did.

Once Jesus emptied himself, He depended on the Holy Spirit to fill Him and to empower him. Similarly, once we empty ourselves we are to depend on God who will then fill us with Holy Spirit. Not that we didn't have Holy Spirit but that the power of the Spirit becomes real to us.

THE POWER OF CROSS

But of him are ye in Christ Jesus, who of God is made unto us wisdom, and righteousness, and sanctification, and redemption: (1 Corinthians 1:30)

The power of cross will be evident in the lives of those who seek salvation in obedience to what Lord Jesus did for them. Adam and Eve ate of the forbidden tree and the curse followed. The ground for man sake was cursed; to the woman, the LORD Said, that she will bear children in pain. The serpent, which was subtle among all the beasts of the field, was cursed to crawl on its belly whole of its life, for deceiving the man and the woman. There is no salvation for the devil, which in the form of serpent deceived Adam and Eve. But on man and woman the Lord had compassion and reconciled them to Himself through His Son. Lord Jesus died on that tree of curse bearing our sins, in order that we may receive salvation.

The LORD God in His mercy sent His own Son to this world and died on the cross. He was buried and rose from the dead on the third day, and later after forty days He ascended into heaven.

Four blessings come from the power of the cross. Jesus by His birth in the form of a servant and in the likeness of man, who died on the cross is made unto us

SANCTIFICATION

1. Wisdom from God
2. Righteousness
3. Sanctification
4. Redemption

CHAPTER 7
NO ONE IS PERFECT.

"And be found in him, not having mine own righteousness, which is of the law, but that which is through the faith of Christ, the righteousness which is of God by faith" (Philippians 3:9)

A person's efforts to gain salvation and imputation of righteousness by good works and by being obedient to the Old Testament laws and commandments would be futile. Failure to keep one law is tantamount to breaking all the laws. The law points guilt of a person and never saves him. It is the blood of Lord Jesus Christ alone that cleanses a sinner of his/her sins.

Apostle Paul repeatedly wrote this fact in his epistles. He was happy that the righteousness that was imputed to him was not through the good works that he did, but through the faith in Jesus Christ. He was happy that the Old Testament law did not provide him the blessedness of being called as righteous. Also, his own good works could not provide him salvation. He was happy to know the truth that he was righteous because it was bestowed on him though faith in God. He was also happy to know the fact about his resurrection.

In the epistle to Philippians 3:13-14 Paul says that he does not want to count himself as having become perfect. He realizes that the purpose of his calling to serve Lord Jesus Christ was not fulfilled. There was always something short of expectation in him, and the need was always there to go beyond what he has already achieved. There was always still some area where he needed to be perfect. His message to us is clear that it is not possible for any man to become perfect, but his message is that one can do one's best to become perfect. It was just as he himself failed in his ventures, and, therefore, he desires that everyone would press on further, just as he would do, to achieve goals to please God who called him through Lord Jesus Christ.

It is, therefore, apt for every child of God not to grumble when he/she faces any suffering, but rejoice in God because every child of God will be heir of God and joint-heir with Lord Jesus Christ. Paul said that he did not reckon his sufferings could be compared with the abundant blessings he would receive in eternity. He goes on to give us the blessed hope that our sufferings are not so intense when they are to stand in comparison with the glory that would be revealed to us.(Romans 8:17-18)

"I press toward the mark for the prize of the high calling of God in Christ Jesus" (Philippians 3:14)";

ABRAHAM FALTERED

We see in the following exposition that Abram, whose name God changed as "Abraham" feared and attempted to escape from trouble. Before we go into meditating on this thought let us recollect a verse from New Testament.

2 Timothy 3:16 reads...

SANCTIFICATION

"All scripture is given by inspiration of God, and is profitable for doctrine, for reproof, for correction, for instruction in righteousness..."

 Now, here is the message from Genesis Chapter 20

 After living for twenty years in Mamre Abram sojourned to Gerar. Abram was also called sojourner. He moved from one place to another. We are also sojourners on this earth looking forward to reaching heaven, which is our final destination. When Abram moved from Mamre to Gerar, he was afraid for some time and tried to lie. That appears to us as unbecoming of his stature as the father of faith. It also renders him the character of cowardice. At a time when Sarai, whose name God changed later as "Sarah", was with a child, a promised seed in her womb, he asked her to say that she was his sister. He was worried more about his own life than living up to the truth.

Abram's own words say: "And yet indeed she is my sister; she is the daughter of my father, but not the daughter of my mother; and she became my wife. (Genesis 20:12)"

Yet, since he married her she was his wife. In his attempt to escape from trouble he said to her that she may tell Abimelech that she was his sister. Because of the fear Abram had Abimelech, the king of Gerar excels in character. The one who was about to commit sin is restored. Abimelech sent for Sarai, and took her to his house with a sinful desire to the take her to his bed. Note that usually one sin paves the way for another. It is indeed disastrous, especially when the sin of God's child paves the way for ungodly to commit sin. Let us, as the children of God, examine ourselves, if our ways are leading others to commit sins.

Because God made covenant with Abram He intervened and prevented the ugliest situation to come up. Psalmist asserts in Psalm 105:13–15 "When they went from one nation to another, from one kingdom to another people; He suffered no man to do them wrong: yea, he reproved kings for their sakes; saying, touch not mine anointed, and do my prophets no harm.

"And the LORD plagued Pharaoh and his house with great plagues because of Sarai Abram's wife" (Genesis 12:17)

God appeared to Abimelech, King of Gerar, in a dream and gave him warning that he was going to commit sin. God revealed to Abhimelech that Sarai was Abram's wife. He also gets warning that if he forces her into illegal relationship he will face death. Abimelech pleads innocent before God and implores for mercy. He prays that he and his nation may not be punished. God grants Abimelech his petition and imputes him no sin.

One aspect that needs to be noted here is that a great deal of sin was devised but it was not executed. More often than not, God restrains people to commit sin.

No temptation is beyond the control of men, and in fact in every situation God provides a way out. It is by our willful act that we fall in to sin, or lead others into sin. In situations where we choose to fall willfully into sin against the will of God we are responsible and accountable. Let us be careful.

"There hath no temptation taken you but such as is common to man: but God is faithful, who will not suffer you to be tempted above that ye are able; but will with the temptation also make a way to escape, that ye may be able to bear it" (1 Corinthians 10:13)

MOSES FALTERED

"Now the man Moses was very meek, above all the men which were upon the face of the earth" (Numbers 12:3)

Moses was very meek among all the men that were upon the face of the earth. He was an instrument reflecting the glory of God just as mirror would reflect the image of man. The only time the mirror attracts attention of the user is when it is dirty. Moses faithfully obeyed God's commands and interceded with Him on behalf of Israelites several times on their journey from Egypt to Canaan. He did not attempt to draw attention to himself but spoke the word of God and exalted His name. But then Moses showed his weakness just as any one of us would do and he was overtaken by his anger towards the murmuring Israelites. He smote the rock twice at Kadesh against the word of the LORD who commanded him to speak to the rock to bring forth water. Under the pressure of Israelites and in anger Moses asked Israelites if he and Aaron should fetch them water out of the rock and then he smote the rock twice. Indeed, water came forth out of the rock and not only congregation drank water but the beasts also drank the water. But the LORD was angry with Moses for his disobedience and said to him that he will not see the Promised Land.

It was, indeed, a trying situation for Moses, whom God called as His servant faithful in His entire house (Numbers 12:7). Miriam, sister of Moses and Aaron spoke against Moses about his prophecy. Miriam was known as prophetess, who sang along with other women unto the LORD for the victory He gave to the

SANCTIFICATION

children of Israel over Pharaoh and His army at
the Red Sea (Exodus 15:20-21).

But then, the LORD did not take it lightly when
she spoke against Moses, the LORD's servant.
The LORD spoke to Moses and to Aaron and to
Miriam and called them to come out of the
tabernacle of the congregation. When they
came out of the tabernacle of the
congregation, the LORD came down in the
pillar of cloud and stood in the door of the
tabernacle. He then called specifically Aaron
and Miriam and said to them that He speaks to
prophets in visions and in dreams but to
Moses he spoke mouth to mouth.

That shows the LORD's intimacy with Moses,
who was His trusted and loved servant. Then
the LORD questioned their daring attitude of
questioning the authority of Moses and
thereafter His anger kindled against Miriam
and she became leprous, white as snow. Aaron
was wonder-struck and addressed Moses as
'lord' and prayed to him that they spoke
foolishly and requested him not to lay the sin
upon them. Moses intervened on behalf of

SANCTIFICATION

them with the LORD and prayed to Him to heal
Miriam. The LORD heard the cry of Moses and
said Miriam be shut out from the camp for
seven days and accordingly she was shut out
for seven days from the camp of Israelites.

The children of Israel stayed until Miriam came
again into their midst. Miriam was healed and
they started their journey again (Numbers
12:1–16).

 Many a time believers speak against the
servants of Lord and after a lapse of time they
see that they are chastised by God and then
they realize that God dealt with them severely
for speaking or working against the servants
of the Lord. God is compassionate to answer
the prayers of the servants of the Lord to bring
mitigation of the chastisement the Lord
imposed on the offenders.

 When the children of Israel reached Kadesh
Miriam died and was buried there. There was
no water in that place for the congregation.
The children of Israel gathered together

Leslie M. John   *Page 69*

against Moses and against Aaron and insulted Moses.

They asked to Moses if he desired that they and their cattle should die in the wilderness that he brought them into wilderness. They spoke that it was not a place of seed, or of figs, or of vines or of pomegranates as if they had all these luxuries while they were slaves in Egypt for four hundred and thirty years.

The children of Israel saw the miracles of God during their journey. They saw how Red Sea was parted and they walked on the dry ground in the midst of the Red Sea. They had sweet water at "Marah", they enjoyed the protection of the LORD by pillar of fire during night and pillar of cloud during day and yet they complained in Kadesh that they did not have vine or pomegranates.

This is classic example of every believer in Christ. Even though we all enjoy the blessings of God ever since we are delivered from the bondage of slavery under sin, at times we cry out to God that we do not have pleasures of the sort of vine or pomegranates, which the Israelites complained of. We forget that we were under the bondage of sin but God delivered us from sin. We tend to forget that Satan had control over us and was leading us to destruction and death, but when we are saved and heading towards our eternal abode we tend to look back at our past life when we had worldly pleasures to enjoy.

The result of their murmuring and not trusting God none but Caleb and Joshua of the generation that left Egypt entered Canaan the Promised Land. Moses died when he was an hundred and twenty years old in the land of Moab according to the word of the LORD and he was buried in a valley in the land of Moab over against Bethpeor but no body knows unto this day where his sepulcher is.

When he died his eye was not dim, nor the efficiency and power of his natural force diminished. The children of Israel mourned his death for thirty days. According to Jude, the servant of Jesus Christ and brother of James, Michael the archangel contended with devil about the body of Moses and instead of rebuking the devil he pronounced that God may rebuke the devil. It was not because Michael the archangel could not rebuke the devil or feared the devil but Michael the archangel feared God. (Deuteronomy 34:5-8, Jude 1:9)

 The Lord gave a very prominent place for Moses in eternity. In the transfiguration of Lord Jesus Christ before Peter, James and John the Lord's face shone as the sun and his raiment was white as the light. "...And, behold, there appeared unto them Moses and Elias talking with him" (Matthew 17:1-3)

 Apostle Paul describes our hope in Lord Jesus Christ in his first epistle to Corinthians chapter 15:51-54 that we shall not all sleep but shall be changed and in a moment of twinkling of an eye we shall put on immortality.

ELIJAH DISAPPOINTED

And Elijah the Tishbite, [who was] of the inhabitants of Gilead, said unto Ahab, [As] the LORD God of Israel liveth, before whom I

SANCTIFICATION

stand, there shall not be dew nor rain these
years, but according to my word. 1 Kings 17:1

God sent Elijah the Prophet to teach Ahab and
his people a lesson to show that He is the God
of gods and idol worship is abomination to
him. King Ahab, son of Omri, ruled Samaria in
Israel for twenty two years and did evil in the
sight of the LORD.

Ahab set up an altar for an idol in the temple
at Samaria and provoked the LORD more than
any other kings of Israel that ruled before.
Elijah took the name of the living LORD God of
Israel and said to Ahab there shall neither be
dew nor will it rain in that land.

The LORD said to Elijah to hide in the eastern
region by the brook of Cherith that is before
Jordan, where God would provide him drink
and feed him food by ravens. Elijah did as God
commanded him and ravens brought him
bread and flesh in the morning and flesh in
the evening and he drank from he brook at
Cherith until the brook dried up for want of
rains in the land.

SANCTIFICATION

The LORD said to Elijah to arise and go to Zarephath in Zidon and dwell there and a widow would provide him food and water.

Elijah did as the LORD told him and went to the widow woman at Zarephath, where the widow was gathering sticks. She and her son were living a poor life in those days when it did not rain. Elijah asked her to fetch him little water in a vessel for a drink and as she was going to fetch water for him, he said to her to bring little bread.

The woman said to him that she does not have bread but has little meal and little oil and that she was gathering sticks so that she may make food for her and her son and eat and live. Elijah the prophet assured her that her food and oil will not cease. In such trial times as these are for the widow woman she provided food and water to the prophet.

And it came to pass after these things, [that] the son of the woman, the mistress of the house, fell sick and his sickness was so sore, that there was no breath left in him. And she said unto Elijah, What have I to do with thee, O thou man of God? art thou come unto me to call my sin to remembrance, and to slay my son? 1 Kings 17:17-18

It so happened that the widow's son fell sick and died. The woman was sore with Elijah and asked him what harm she did to him that her son died and if he went there to call for remembrance of her sin. Elijah had compassion on her and asked her to bring her son and when she brought her son to him, he took her son out of her bosom and took him and laid him on his bed. Elijah stretched himself upon widow's son three times and prayed to the LORD to let the child's soul return to him.

The LORD heard the voice of Elijah and gave life to the son of the widow. Elijah gave the living child to the widow woman, who trusted in the man of God and acknowledged him as the man of God.

ELIJAH'S CHALLENGE

And it came to pass [after] many days, that the word of the LORD came to Elijah in the third year, saying, Go, shew thyself unto Ahab and I will send rain upon the earth 1 Kings 18:1

The LORD said to Elijah to go to Ahab the king and God shall send rain to the earth and Elijah did as the LORD told him. There was a devout man, who was governor in the house of Ahab and his name was Obadiah, who greatly feared the LORD and hid one hundred prophets in two separate groups of fifty each to save them from the wrath of Jezebel, a wicked wife of Ahab determined to kill Gods' children. Wife and husband were both working against the will of God and it troubled the LORD to the extent of showing his strength and power to save his children from his wrath.

It was it this time that the LORD told Elijah to present before this wicked king, Ahab, who set up idols for worshipping in order that his people in the land may not worship the living God. In the midst of severe famine in that land of Samaria, Ahab said to Obadiah to go into his land and find if there is any water any where and find grass to save the horses from death and not lose all the beasts.

And Ahab said unto Obadiah, Go into the land, unto all fountains of water, and unto all brooks: peradventure we may find grass to save the horses and mules alive, that we lose not all the beasts (1 Kings 18:5) Ahab and Obadiah went on journey in two separate directions to find the water and grass. Strangely enough Ahab and Obadiah went in search of food and water for Ahab's cattle instead of finding food and water for the natives of the kingdom. Their thoughts were, indeed, evil.

Obadiah may have been obedient to Ahab because, even though he greatly feared God and a devout man, he was a trusted governor of his house. On the way of Obadiah there was this man of God, Elijah. Obadiah saw him and fell on his face in obeisance to him and inquired of him if he was his lord Elijah.

SANCTIFICATION

The prophet answered Obadiah that he was
Elijah and said to him to go to Ahab and let
him know that he was there. Obadiah was
scared to hear this from Elijah and asked him
if was out there to see that he gets killed by
Ahab and get himself killed as well inasmuch
as the king took an oath to kill Elijah. Obadiah
also feared his destiny if he went and told
Ahab whereabouts of Elijah and in the
meanwhile the Spirit of the LORD carried Elijah
to a place that Obadiah did not know.

Obadiah thought that Ahab would kill him if
peradventure that kind of situation would
come to pass. In an acknowledgement that he
feared Elijah all his life, Obadiah wondered if
Elijah did not hear that he hid hundred
prophets, (fifty each separately), from the
wrath of Jezebel, who slew the prophets of the
LORD, and fed them with bread and water.

Elijah said that his whereabouts to be
disclosed to Ahab. Obadiah feared that king
Ahab would kill him if he disclosed that Elijah
was there to see him. Elijah assures him that
as the LORD lives, he will surely show himself

to Ahab that day and, therefore, Obadiah went and told Ahab about Elijah's whereabouts, and his intention of seeing Ahab. And Elijah said, As the LORD of hosts liveth, before whom I stand, I will surely shew myself unto him to day. So Obadiah went to meet Ahab, and told him: and Ahab went to meet Elijah (1 Kings 18:15-16)

And it came to pass, when Ahab saw Elijah, that Ahab said unto him, Art thou he that troubleth Israel? And he answered, I have not troubled Israel but thou, and thy father's house, in that ye have forsaken the commandments of the LORD, and thou hast followed Baalim (1 Kings 18:17-18)After hearing this from Obadiah, Ahab saw Elijah, and asked him if he was the one who was troubling Israel.

Elijah denies and tells him that it was not he that was troubling Israel, but king Ahab, who was troubling Israelites. Elijah said to him that Ahab was leading them away from truth of the LORD by asking them obey Baal, an idol and worship that idol instead of worshipping the living God. Elijah told Ahab that the latter's father's house have forsaken the commandments of the LORD and followed Baalim.

Inasmuch as Ahab was following Baalim, Elijah threw gauntlets at him for a great showdown to see the power of the LORD in the face of nothingness of idols and their power wherein Ahab and his family greatly relied. Ahab and his family not only disobeyed the LORD but also made the whole nation to disobey the LORD. He forced them to forget about the commandments of the LORD and in addition his wicked wife was set out herself and slew the LORD's prophets.

Now therefore send, and gather to me all Israel unto mount Carmel, and the prophets of Baal four hundred and fifty, and the prophets of the groves four hundred, which eat at Jezebel's table (1 Kings 18:19)This enraged the LORD and sent Elijah for a showdown of His strength and power. Therefore, Elijah said to Ahab to gather to him all Israel on the mount Carmel and also the four hundred and fifty he prophets of 'Baal', and the four hundred prophets of the 'groves' that ate at the table of his wife, Jezebel. Ahab agreed and sent word to gather all the children and the said number of prophets on the Mount Carmel. When they are all gathered, Elijah asked them how long they would have two opinions about following the real God. Elijah said that if they trusted the LORD they may follow the LORD or they may follow Baal. <br/ />On refusal by Ahab to believe in the living God Elijah decided for the big showdown. Elijah said to them that he was alone standing on behalf of the LORD presenting himself as the prophet of the LORD as against four hundred fifty men standing as prophets of Baal.

Let them therefore give us two bullocks and let them choose one bullock for themselves, and cut it in pieces, and lay it on wood, and put no fire under: and I will dress the other bullock, and lay it on wood, and put no fire under (1 Kings 18:23)

Elijah challenged the prophets of Baal to have one bullock, cut into pieces, lay the pieces on

SANCTIFICATION

the wood, and put no fire under the wood, but call for their gods to consume the offering. He would then dress his bullock, cut it into pieces and place the pieces on the wood and put no fire and call his God to consume the offering and this challenge pleased the children of Israel. His challenge was to prove that the God of Israel is the living and true God.

Elijah said if the gods of the prophets of Baal came and consumed the offering, he and the children of Israel would believe that their gods are real gods. Elijah offered the prophets of Baal to have the priority of calling their gods to consume the offering.

The prophets of Baal agreed and had their bullock cut into pieces and after placing them on the wood with no fire under called on the name of Baal, their god, morning until noon desperately crying to hear their voice but there was no response from their god. And they took the bullock which was given them, and they dressed it, and called on the name of Baal from morning even until noon, saying, O Baal, hear us.

SANCTIFICATION

But there was no voice, nor any that answered.
And they leaped upon the altar which was
made. (1 Kings 18:26) Elijah mocked at the
prophets of Baal and asked them to cry loud
because, according to them, he is a god. Their
god may be talking to some one or is pursuing
on his journey or he may be sleeping that he
needs to be awakened.

And it came to pass at noon, that Elijah
mocked them, and said, Cry aloud: for he is a
god either he is talking, or he is pursuing, or
he is in a journey, or peradventure he
sleepeth, and must be awaked (1 Kings 18:27)
They cried aloud more and more and cut
themselves with knives and lancets until their
blood gushed out from their bodies.

They cried until evening and even then their
god had no ears to hear and did not answer
their prayers nor had any compassion on the
blood they shed for him. Their god did not
respond to his children who shed their blood
for him he did not help them in their dire need
of a great showdown where Elijah had thrown
gauntlets before them to prove their god is

SANCTIFICATION

true god. Their god could not come to their rescue nor did he save them.

And they cried aloud, and cut themselves after their manner with knives and lancets, till the blood gushed out upon them (1 Kings 18:28)Baal worshippers shed blood for their god! But our Savior shed blood for us.

At the end of the day the worshippers of Baal had nothing but their own blood shed for their god and tired bodies. Is it not worth pondering that their god could not have compassion on them even when they shed their precious blood for him, just in contrast to our living God, who sent his one and only son, Jesus Christ, who shed his precious blood for our sake, so that whoever believes in him shall have eternal life and will not perish?

It is our living God, who loved us first, not that we loved him first that he sent his one and only son Jesus Christ for the remission of our sins. Elijah said to the people to go near him and he repaired the altar of the LORD that was broken down and took twelve stones according to the number of the tribes of Jacob, whom God loved and renamed him as Israel. With the stones he built an altar in the name of the LORD and made around the altar a trench of the size that would contain two measures of seed. He set the wood in order and laid the pieces of the bullock that he cut and ordered the children of Israel, to pour four barrels of water thrice upon the burnt sacrifice, and on the wood so that the water ran round the altar and in addition, he filled the trench with water.

It was at the time of the offering of the evening sacrifice that Elijah came near and prayed to the LORD, that the LORD being the God of Abraham, Isaac, and Israel, let it be known that day that he was the God of Israel, and Elijah was his servant. Elijah prayed, Hear me, O LORD, hear me, that this people may know that thou art the LORD God, and that thou hast turned their heart back again. (1 Kings 18:37 KJV) and the LORD answered Elijah,

"Then the fire of the LORD fell, and consumed the burnt sacrifice, and the wood, and the

stones, and the dust, and licked up the water that was in the trench". (1 Kings 18:38)

Then the fire of the LORD fell, and consumed the burnt sacrifice, and the wood, and the stones, and the dust, and licked up the water that was in the trench. And when all the people saw it, they fell on their faces: and they said, The LORD, he is the God the LORD, he is the God (1 Kings 18:38-39)

This showdown ended really to prove that the LORD was the God of Abraham, Isaac, and Israel, and all the people that saw this miracle fell on their faces and acknowledged that the LORD, He is the God the LORD, he is the God.... Elijah did not end it all there but instructed that the prophets of Baal be taken making sure that not one of them escapes punishment. He brought them to the brook of Kishon and slew them there.

Elijah, then told Ahab to get up, eat and drink and there was sound of abundance of rain. As Ahab went to eat and drink, Elijah went on to the top of Mount Carmel and prayed to God with his face between his knees casting himself down on to the earth.

While praying Elijah, asked his servant to go and see if there was rain coming down. The servant went and came and said, there was no rain, and Elijah did this seven times and lo, there arose a small cloud out the sea like a man's hand. Elijah said to his servant to go Ahab and say about all these happenings, and prepare for himself a chariot and have a ride to celebrate happiness, and let not the rain stop him. In the mean while there came down heavy down pour from heaven, and Ahab rode and went to Jezreel. Elijah had the blessings of having the LORD's hand upon him and, therefore, he also girded his loins up and ran before Ahab the entrance of Jezreel. Thus the LORD's name was glorified and every body trusted in the living God.

JEZEBEL IN ACTION

Seventh king in Israel was Ahab who was the son of Omri who reigned over Israel in Samaria for twenty two years. Ahab did greater evil than that of any one of his predecessors in the sight of the Lord. As if the evil that he did in the sight of the LORD was not enough he took Jezebel the daughter of Ethbaal king of Zidonians as his wife. Zidonians were the offspring of Sidon, son of Canaan.

"And Canaan begat Sidon his firstborn, and Heth" (Genesis 10:15) If we trace back to Canaan's lineage he is the son of Ham who saw the nakedness of his father Noah who was drunk. Ham went and told his brothers who walked backwards without seeing the nakedness of their father and covered him. When Noah came to senses from his intoxication he knew what Ham did to him and cursed him saying he will be servant of servants of his brothers(Cf. Genesis 9:19-25).

Ahab married and had very bad ties with the lineage of Cursed Canaan. Ahab's wife Jezebel was wicked woman who brought idol worship into Israel. Not only Ahab and Jezebel worshipped Baal but they introduced Baal worship in Israel. Jezebel was the architect of Baal worship in Israel. Ahab reared up an altar for Baal in the house of Baal and thus Ahab provoked God of Israel to anger more than any one of his predecessors. (Cf. 1 Kings 16:29-34)

It came to pass that there was a man named Naboth, a Jezrelite, who had a vineyard that was in Jezreel. The vineyard was very close by the palace of Ahab, who once spoke to Nabath and said to him sell the vineyard to him for a price or have another vineyard at another place as compensation.

Naboth did not agree to such proposal because he had it from his forefathers as inheritance. Ahab was displeased with Naboth and was sad. Ahab's wicked wife Jezebel came to him and asked him as to why he was so sad.

Ahab said to Jezebel that he asked Naboth to sell his vineyard to him or have another vineyard as compensation but he refused saying that it was an inheritance from his forefathers. Jezebel thought it legitimate to grab Naboth's property because her husband is king over the land.

SANCTIFICATION

She thought it is legitimate to have a citizen's property even when the citizen refuses to sell it. She not only thought it so but adopted very wicked way of grabbing Naboth's vineyard.

And Jezebel his wife said unto him, Dost thou now govern the kingdom of Israel? arise, and eat bread, and let thine heart be merry: I will give thee the vineyard of Naboth the Jezreelite. So she wrote letters in Ahab's name, and sealed them with his seal, and sent the letters unto the elders and to the nobles that were in his city, dwelling with Naboth (1 Kings 21:7-8)

Ahab's wife Jezebel said to him to get up, eat bread and be merry because he was the king over the kingdom of Israel and that she would take charge of solving the problem. Jezebel wrote letters in Ahab's name, sealed them with his seal and sent the letter to the elders and to the nobles in the city living with Naboth. In the letters she wrote to the elders and nobles to proclaim a fast and set Naboth on high.

SANCTIFICATION

It is usual in those days that the criminal is placed in high place to be seen.

Jezebel apparently made him by her letters to appear Naboth like a criminal although he was exercising what was within his rights. According to her letter two men who were sons of Belial to witness against him that he blasphemed God and the king. (sons of Belial means the sons of worthless men [Cf. Judges 20:13, 2 Samuel 23:6, 2 Corinthians 6:15).

After willful and false declaration of Naboth as criminal the elders and the nobles were to stone him to death. The men of city, the elders and the nobles did just as Jezebel wrote treacherously in the name of her husband and stoned Naboth unto death.

Jezebel went to Ahab and said to him that Naboth is dead and he may go and take possession of his vineyard. While Naboth was on his way to take possession of the vineyard Elijah came to him with the word of the LORD and said to him: ...

SANCTIFICATION

Thus saith the LORD, In the place where dogs licked the blood of Naboth shall dogs lick thy blood, even thine. (1 Kings 21:19 b) Elijah said of Jezebel saying ...The dogs shall eat Jezebel by the wall of Jezreel (1 Kings 21:23 b) Elijah's prophecy was that Ahab and his posterity to be rooted out fully just as the families of Jeroboam and of Baasha were rooted out. (1 Kings 14:11, 16:4 and 1 Kings 21:22) and dogs shall eat the dead bodies in the city and the fowls of the air shall eat that die in the fields because Ahab sold himself to wickedness in the sight of the LORD and Jezebel his wife stirred him up to execute the wickedness.

Ahab did abomination in the sight of the LORD in following idols.

God hated Amorites and He compares Ahab's idol worship to that of worship of idols by the Amorites. Nevertheless, as Ahab repented of his sin by putting on sackcloth upon his flesh and fasted, the word of the LORD came to Elijah and the LORD said through him that the

SANCTIFICATION

evil would come upon not in his days but in the days of his sons (Cf. 1 Kings 21:24–29).

So Ahab slept with his fathers and Ahaziah his son reigned in his stead (1 Kings 22:40) In the days of Elisha the prophet Jehu was anointed as king over Israel. Elisha said to Jehu that he shall smite the house of Ahab that the LORD may avenge the blood of His servants the prophets and the blood of all the servants of the LORD at the hands of Jezebel. He also said that the dogs shall eat Jezebel in the portion of Jezreeel and there shall be no one to bury her (Ref: 2 Kings 9:7–10).

At the instructions of Jehu three eunuchs threw Jezebel from out of the window and some of her blood was sprinkled on the wall and on the horses and he trode her under foot and the prophecy of Elijah was fulfilled. And he said, Throw her down.

So they threw her down: and some of her blood was sprinkled on the wall, and on the horses: and he trode her under foot. And when he was come in, he did eat and drink, and said, Go, see now this cursed woman, and bury her: for she is a king's daughter. And they went to bury her: but they found no more of her than the skull, and the feet, and the palms of her hands. Wherefore they came again, and told him. And he said, This is the word of the LORD, which he spake by his servant Elijah the Tishbite, saying, In the portion of Jezreel shall dogs eat the flesh of Jezebel (2 Kings 9:33-36)

Immediately after an amazing victory Israel scored over the prophets of Baal at the Mount Carmel with the help of the Almighty God through the chosen prophet of the LORD, Elijah the Tishbite, the prophet himself fell into disappointment and fear at the threat of Jezebel the wicked wife of Ahab.

Jezebel heard about the insult the prophets of Baal and their god Baal faced. Jezebel swore and threatened to kill Elijah. Then Jezebel sent a messenger unto Elijah, saying, So let the gods do to me, and more also, if I make not thy life as the life of one of them by to morrow about this time. (1 Kings 19:2) On hearing from her husband that the prophets of Baal were killed by Elijah Jezebel was furious on Elijah and sent messengers seeking his blood. She took an oath on the names of her gods that if she did not kill Elijah by the next morning her gods would be free to take her life.

ELIJAH COMFORTED

Sometimes it so happens that the child of God faces uncertainties in his/her life and loses confidence in himself even though he had tremendous success in the past. It may be because he faced a threat from somebody, or a small failure after scoring a victory. But then God sends his angels and comforts his children. Elijah faced discouragement when such great threat came from the wicked woman Jezebel, who took an oath to kill him.

Elijah ran for his life and went to Beersheba that belongs to Judah and left his servant there. Thereafter, he went and sat under a juniper tree and said to himself that it would be better if he died and then prayed to God to take his life saying he was not better than his fathers. As he was lying under the juniper tree an angel of the Lord came to him, touched him and told him to get up and eat. And as he lay and slept under a juniper tree, behold, then an angel touched him, and said unto him, Arise and eat. And he looked, and, behold, there was a cake baken on the coals, and a cruse of water at his head. And he did eat and drink, and laid him down again. And the angel of the LORD came again the second time, and touched him, and said, Arise and eat because the journey is too great for thee. (1 Kings 19:5-7)

And he looked, and, behold, there was a cake baken on the coals, and a cruse of water at his head. And he did eat and drink, and laid him down again (1 Kings 19:6) When Elijah was worried the first thing that an angel of the Lord did to him was to feed him food. Elijah found a baked cake and a jar of water at his head. He got up and ate and drank and laid down again in disappointment in spite of the assurance he found in the angel of the Lord.

SANCTIFICATION

The threat from Jezebel was so great that Elijah, who did himself confidently several miracles through the help of God, now finds hard to come out the depression of the supposedly an imminent danger. This reminds of the children of God, who face such challenges in life and get disappointed at few threats or few dangers that appear to harm them. In spite of the fact that God is with us some times we face discouragement.

But then, God does not leave us alone in disappointment. He sends his angels repeatedly to infuse in our hearts confidence and to advise us to take courage. Fear ye not therefore, ye are of more value than many sparrows (Matthew 10:31 KJV)

The angel of the LORD went to Elijah second time, touched him and told him to eat because the journey is too great for him. Elijah arose and ate and drank and received strength and with that strength he traveled for forty days and forty nights and reached the Horeb the mount of God.

SANCTIFICATION

Elijah went into a cave and lodged there and at that time the word of the LORD came to him and asked what he was doing there. Elijah spoke out from the bottom of his heart and said that he had been working so zealously for the LORD in spite of the fact that Israel had forsaken His covenant, thrown down His altars and slain His prophets with the sword, and yet his own life is in danger and they seek his life. The LORD said to Elijah to go and stand on the mount and see when He passes by. As Elijah was watching carefully a great and strong wind rent the mountains and broke the rocks in to pieces before the LORD but the LORD was not there.

Thereafter Elijah saw an earthquake, and a fire but the LORD was not in them as well. But there came a small and still voice unto him and asked Elijah as to what he was doing there. Elijah repeated his saying that he was working so zealously for the LORD, even when the children of Israel had forsakes the LORD's covenant, thrown down His altars and slew His prophets and yet he was all alone working for him and his life was in danger.

SANCTIFICATION

The LORD spoke to him and said to him to return to the nearby villages of Damascus and do certain important works for Him. And the LORD said unto him, Go, return on thy way to the wilderness of Damascus: and when thou comest, anoint Hazael to be king over Syria: And Jehu the son of Nimshi shalt thou anoint to be king over Israel: and Elisha the son of Shaphat of Abelmeholah shalt thou anoint to be prophet in thy room. And it shall come to pass, that him that escapeth the sword of Hazael shall Jehu slay: and him that escapeth from the sword of Jehu shall Elisha slay. (1 Kings 19:15-17)

The LORD also said to him that there were seven thousand in Israel, who have not kneeled down to Baal. God's work does not stop at one man's disappointment nor does he leave the one, who is disappointed. God takes of his work through Elisha, who comes after Elijah.

The LORD comforted Elijah and took care of His work as well. In the subsequent chapters we read that Elijah was caught up in to heaven.

SANCTIFICATION

Let the name of the Lord be glorified. In hardships and difficult situations God sends comfort through some one or some situation. When the ship in which Paul and others were sailing had a wreck Paul comforts all.

DAVID FALTERED

David's Psalm116 encourages believers to ponder life in retrospect and the deliverance the LORD wrought upon them from their distress, sin and iniquities.

Not once but several times in his life David was fleeing from his pursuers like Saul and then later in his life from his own son Absalom. In all the occasions when he was fleeing from his persecutors he depended on God for help and his prayers and supplications were answered. Because David asked forgiveness from God He dealt with all his trials and tribulations compassionately and took care of them and forgave him. The LORD called David, a man after His own heart. It is so precious to be called by God as a man after His own heart. David was not perfect in his life. His adultery with Bathsheba and killing of her husband Uriah had gone on record never to be erased. He numbered his own army once pointing to the fact that his reliance on the LORD diminished. Yet, he was called a man of after God's own heart not because God approved his iniquities, sin and his pride but because David repented of his sin and sought mercy from the LORD.

David says he loved the LORD because He heard his voice and his supplications. The LORD inclined His ear to him and, therefore, he committed to call on the LORD as long as he lived. He recollects that sorrows of death compassed him, and the pains of hell got hold of him. He called upon the name of the LORD to deliver his soul when he was in trouble and sorrow and the LORD delivered him because the LORD was gracious and merciful. David assures, thereafter, that the Lord preserves the humble.

The LORD was good to him when he confessed his sin to Him as we read in Psalm 51, It was when Nathan the prophet went to him and showed him how he has flawed in his walk with God. When the LORD gave him Kingship and the authority to rule over whole of Israel, he fell into his fleshly desire. David was highly remorseful of his sin and made available his psalm of confession to be sung by the chief musician aloud before the congregation.

GOD FORGAVE DAVID

David sought God's mercy and prayed to God to blot out his transgressions. He sought multitude of tender mercies and loving kindness from the LORD. David acknowledged his iniquity and prayed for his cleansing. He realized that by yielding to his fleshly desires he sinned against the LORD and done evil.

David also remembered the very condition of every man born on this earth. He says in sin did his mother conceive him and he was shaped in iniquity. This is the condition of every human being born on this earth. .

Behold, I was shapen in iniquity; and in sin did my mother conceive me. (Psalms 51:5)

SANCTIFICATION

Nevertheless, God looks at the heart of a man and searches his thoughts. Man is wicked in his very thoughts and unless he seeks the holy presence of the Lord in his heart he would slowly but surely slide into irretrievable situation of being in sin.

Apostle Paul writes that we all have sinned and fell short of the glory of God. The wages of sin is death but the gift of God is eternal life through Jesus Christ our Lord. There is surely a way to be saved from sin and receive the gift of eternal life.

"That if thou shalt confess with thy mouth the Lord Jesus, and shalt believe in thine heart that God hath raised him from the dead, thou shalt be saved. For with the heart man believeth unto righteousness; and with the mouth confession is made unto salvation" Romans 10:29, 30

SOLOMON FALTERED

"Thou shalt have no other gods before me" Exodus 20:3

Leslie M. John   *Page 103*

SANCTIFICATION

Contrary to the commandment of the LORD that the children of Israel shall not marry women from the nations i.e. Moabites, Ammonites, Edomites, Zidonians and Hittites nor will they give their women in marriage to them Solomon loved many from those nations of which one was Pharaoh's daughter. God was very clear to the children of Israel that if they go in to them or they come in to them the nations will turn the hearts of the children of Israel to go after their gods. (Ref. 1 Kings Chapter 11)

"And thou take of their daughters unto thy sons, and their daughters go a whoring after their gods, and make thy sons go a whoring after their gods" (Exodus 34:16)

Solomon went after Ashteroth the goddess of the Zidonians and after Milcom the abomination of the Ammonites and he did evil in the sight to the LORD. Solomon's disobedience did not end there but he went ahead infuriating God by building high place for Chemosh, the abomination of Moab , in the hill that is before Jerusalem. How sad it is that he did this before the city on which the LORD had put His own name. He also built high place for Molech, the abomination of Amnon. His strange wives burnt incense before the idols and sacrificed unto the idols which, they worshiped, as their gods.

The result of Solomon's disobedience was seen very quickly in the fall of his kingdom.

Solomon had seven hundred wives, princess and three hundred concubines. God hates idolatry. The idolatry among those in Solomon's period was not new. Jacob spoke the desire of the LORD when he said to his household and to all that were with him to put away the strange gods that were among them and be clean and change their garments. Earlier, Rachel stole the images that were her father's (Ref. Genesis 31:19)

"Then Jacob said unto his household, and to all that were with him, Put away the strange gods that are among you, and be clean, and change your garments" (Genesis 35:2)

SANCTIFICATION

"Thou shalt not make unto thee any graven image, or any likeness of any thing that is in heaven above, or that is in the earth beneath, or that is in the water under the earth" (Exodus 20:4)

The defiance of the LORD's desire was seen when Aaron made a molten calf from the jewelry that he collected from the children of Israel while Moses was still on the Mount Sinai conversing with the LORD. It is so pathetic that Aaron, who stood by Moses when miracles were shown before Pharaoh and who knew very well that it was the God of Abraham, that God of Isaac and the God of Jacob who delivered them from the bondage of slavery under Pharaoh made an image and gave it to them . The people said that it was the idol that delivered them from the bondage of slavery.

After the calf was made the children of Israel said "...These be thy gods, O Israel, which brought thee out of the land of Egypt" (Exodus 32:4). This verse should be read and understood clearly.

"And he received them at their hand, and
fashioned it with a graving tool, after he had
made it a molten calf: and they said, These be
thy gods, O Israel, which brought thee up out
of the land of Egypt" (Exodus 32:4)

However, Aaron built an altar before it and
proclaimed that the next day was the feast of
the LORD and they rose up early on the
morrow and offered burnt offerings and peace
of offerings and rejoiced. That is a clear
indication that the children of Israel did not
forget Jehovah but had a misguided notion
about God of heaven and the gods that they
saw in Egypt. (Ref. Exodus 32:5, 6)

This is the major reason why the children of
Israel were chastised number of times by God
to make them understand that Jehovah is the
true God.

SOLOMON RESTORED

In the Bible we come across several stalwarts
of faith and followers of God erring in their
daily lives. It is not uncommon that men fell
into sin and were forgiven of God. Some of

those who fell from the presence of God and made lasting impression on mankind are as follows:

Adam and Eve transgressed the commandment of God who said to them that they should not eat of the fruit of the tree of the knowledge of good and evil and passed on their Sin to entire mankind. Their folly resulted in knowing that they were naked and needed a covering for their body. Their own efforts of providing covering for their bodies were found short of God's requirements and, therefore, God clothed them with coats of skins. (Ref. Genesis 2:17, 3:21)

Abraham, who was called as man of faith, faltered on one occasion when he said to his wife that she should say that she was his sister when they journeyed toward Gerar. Abimelech, king of Geral took Sarah, but God intervened and no harm was done to Sarah. (Ref. Genesis 20:1–2)

Moses, the faithful servant of the LORD, faltered once when he struck the rock for water instead of speaking to it, and God did not permit him to enter the Promised Land in spite of his ardent prayer request that he may be allowed to see the Promised Land and yet he was found with Lord Jesus Christ during His transfiguration.

"I pray thee, let me go over, and see the good land that [is] beyond Jordan , that goodly mountain, and Lebanon . But the LORD was wroth with me for your sakes, and would not hear me: and the LORD said unto me, Let it suffice thee; speak no more unto me of this matter". Deuteronomy 3:25-26

"And after six days Jesus taketh Peter, James, and John his brother, and bringeth them up into an high mountain apart, And was transfigured before them: and his face did shine as the sun, and his raiment was white as the light. And, behold, there appeared unto them Moses and Elias talking with him". Matthew 17:1-3

David committed adultery with Bathsheba and got her husband killed and yet when he repented God forgave him.

THERE IS FORGIVENESS

The second malefactor on the cross said a simple prayer and Lord Jesus Christ was gracious to him.

"And he said unto Jesus, Lord, remember me when thou comest into thy kingdom. And Jesus said unto him, Verily I say unto thee, To day shalt thou be with me in paradise" Luke 23:42, 43

In the case of Solomon's transgression there was a provision made by God when He said to David that he will chasten him with the rod of men and with the stripes of the children of men but His mercy shall not depart from him. (Ref. 2 Samuel 7:13-15). In addition, many verses from the book of Song of Solomon and the Book of Ecclesiastes; especially the last two verses from the Book of Euclasites reveal that Solomon repented.

"Let us hear the conclusion of the whole matter: Fear God, and keep his commandments: for this [is] the whole [duty] of man. For God shall bring every work into judgment, with every secret thing, whether [it be] good, or whether [it be] evil". Ecclesiastes 12:13-14

In the light of the above facts it can be safely concluded that Solomon is saved by the grace of God.

SECURITY OF SALVATION

Salvation, which is the gift of God, is so precious that once it is given to a believer God can not deny His own love toward us, nor can He deny His love toward His One and only Son, Jesus Christ that He takes back that gift from us.

Romans 6:23 is a very familiar verse in the Bible. There is one great gift that God gave unto us through His One and Only Son Jesus Christ and that gift is the salvation and it is the greatest gift of all. Wages are the earnings for the work done by someone. Bible calls the

SANCTIFICATION

wages of sin is death, but the gift of God is
eternal life through Jesus Christ our Lord.

 The Father in heaven in His mercy sent His
One and Only Son Jesus Christ because He
loved us first, even when we were dead in our
trespasses and saved us by grace.

 Salvation can neither be earned through the
works nor can it be purchased for a price. It is
the gift of God through Lord Jesus Christ. He
paid the price for our sins upon the cross of
Calvary. He shed His precious blood for our
sake and washed our sins in His blood.

The love of God is so great that He found us in
our trespasses and sent His One and Only Son,
Jesus Christ for our sake, that whosoever
believes in Him shall not perish but will have
everlasting life. If we confess our sins, He is
faithful and just to forgive us our sins. He
sought us because He loved us first. We
received salvation not because we loved Him
first, but because He loved us first.

A believer can trust in the words of Lord Jesus
Christ, just as Apostle Paul affirmed in Romans

8:38-39, that neither any one or any act, or any power, can separate us from the love of God, because we are in Christ Jesus and let us, therefore, give thanks unto the Father in heaven, just as Apostle Paul asked us to do in Colossians 1:1-13. God made us partakers in the inheritance of the saints in light and delivered from the power of darkness in order to translate us into the Kingdom of His One and Only Son, Jesus Christ. We believe in the gospel of Jesus Christ and about the eternal life that Jesus promised to us and we are sealed with the Holy Spirit of promise. We are purchased possession of our God so that we may be unto him the praise of his glory. We should bear in mind the hope of our calling, and know "what the riches of the glory of his inheritance in the saints" (Eph.1:13-18)

THE JUDGMENT SEAT OF CHRIST

For we must all appear before the judgment seat of Christ; that every one may receive the things done in his body, according to that he hath done, whether it be good or bad. (2 Corinthians 5:10)

SANCTIFICATION

Every believer has to account for the deeds he has done on this earth in order to receive the rewards at the 'Bema seat of Christ' He shall stand at the judgment seat of Christ also known as 'Bema Seat of Christ' not as an unbeliever to receive judgment for punishment, but for rewards he is entitled for working for the Lord.

During the period of time when the believer is with the Lord and after the rapture, the Lord will honor his servants for the service they rendered unto Him when they were on this earth. We are not to judge our brothers because we shall all stand before the judgment seat of Christ (Rom.14:10).

The time will come when the Lord comes and He brings to the light every hidden things of darkness, and will show the counsels that have taken place in the hearts. While God does this in the presence of every believer at the judgment seat of Christ every man will praise God (1 Cor.4:5)

SANCTIFICATION

Lord Jesus Christ is our life and He will appear in the clouds in glory to receive His own unto Himself and honor them with rewards.⁂

 It is not the Great white Throne judgment, when those, who have not believed in Him, will be judged for their everlasting destiny in the lake of fire along with the Satan and his angels, but the judgment seat of Christ is the raised seat where He sits as the King of kings to administer justice. There shall be no condemnation for the believers, who are in Christ, and who have not walked after the flesh, but sought to walk after the Spirit. (Rom 8:1).

God was in Christ and reconciled us unto Himself, and made us, who have trusted in Him, and confessed our sins to Him, as his heirs and did not impute our trespasses unto us, but washed our sins in the precious blood of Jesus. We are His workmanship, created in Christ unto good works and we stand worthy of our calling and deserve our rewards at the 'Bema Seat of Christ'. It is a blessed hope for believer that he will be honored for putting on

Christ and for living holy life. It is at this time, when we, the believers are with the Lord, that we will be rewarded before He reveals Himself on this earth again.

GREAT TRIBULATION

But pray ye that your flight be not in the winter, neither on the sabbath day: For then shall be great tribulation, such as was not since the beginning of the world to this time, no, nor ever shall be. (Matthew 24:20–21)

Caught in their disbelief Jews have always been waiting for Messiah to come from an earthly King's family. This disbelief in the Messiah, who was their real King, has led them to reject Lord Jesus Christ, the Messiah, as their Savior. Just as a hen gathers her chicken under her wings, God yearned to gather the children of Israel, the blessed generation through, Jesus, who was born in their clan, of the Virgin Mary from the lineage of King David, but they not only rejected Him, but also killed prophets and stoned them, who were sent to them.

SANCTIFICATION

They rejected the true Messiah, Lord Jesus Christ even to the extent that Jesus, who answered a woman, that He was sent unto the lost sheep of Israel, was not received by them. But, when the woman, a gentile, who was praying that her daughter be healed by Him, crying,

"O Lord, thou Son of David; my daughter is grievously vexed with a devil." (Matt 15:22), and had faith in Him saying,

"Truth, Lord: yet the dogs eat of the crumbs which fall from their masters' table". (Matt 15:27),

Jesus had compassion on her and granted answer to her prayer. A gentile received because Jews rejected Him. Apostle Paul writes about this mystery that is revealed in the New Testament about God accepting Gentiles in to the Church. (Ephesians 3:3-9).

The Church consisting of individual members, who have accepted Jesus as their Savior, are therefore, given the privilege over the Jews, and they are 'caught up' when the Lord himself

SANCTIFICATION

'shall descend from heaven with a shout, with the voice of the archangel, and with the trump of God: and the dead in Christ shall rise first: Then we which are alive and remain shall be caught up together with them in the clouds, to meet the Lord in the air: and so shall we ever be with the Lord'. (1 Thessalonians 4:16-17).

The unbelieving Jews and all others, who have not accepted Jesus Christ as their personal Savior will enter into the 70th week of Daniel, as prophesied in Daniel 9:26,27. Those, who are saved, will be with the Lord, when all others, who are not saved that includes the Jews will left- behind to be under the reign of Antichrist.

While the believers are happy with the Lord, and receive their rewards for their good works done on the earth, the unbelievers will be under the reign of Antichrist, who promises them earthly peace, pomp, honor, and wealth. In the middle of the last week (70th week), that is after completion of 3.5 years, their king, the Antichrist, will break the covenant that he made with them, and then will start the 'great tribulation'.

It is at this time that the Jews as prophesied will call upon God to have mercy on them, and God will come their rescue, and every one of them will be saved. Immediately after the tribulation of those days 'great tribulation' are over, 'the sun shall be darkened, and the moon shall not give her light, and the stars shall fall away from heaven and the powers of the heavens shall be shaken'. (Matthew 24:29).

THE JUDGMENT OF THE WICKED

And I saw a great white throne, and him that sat on it, from whose face the earth and the heaven fled away; and there was found no place for them. And I saw the dead, small and great, stand before God; and the books were opened: and another book was opened, which is the book of life: and the dead were judged out of those things which were written in the books, according to their works. (Revelation 20:11 –12)

SANCTIFICATION

This is the 'Great White Throne judgment', which is the final judgment, where every one, whose name is not found in the book of life is judged and 'death and hell will be cast into the lake of fire. This is the second death'. (Rev. 20:14)

CHAPTER 8
THE CHASTISEMENT

"My son, despise not the chastening of the LORD; neither be weary of his correction" (Proverbs 3:11)

None of us would like to suffer pain. However, God allows pain in the lives of those who are called according to His purpose. He, being the Father, called us as His "little children", and His dealing with His children is within His authority; it is the family relationship (cf. 1 John 2:1). He chastens his children, who drift away from His paths, and choose to continue to be in sin. He chastens in order that they may not be lost, but to come back to Him.

Prodigal son wasted his inheritance, and thereafter wished to fill "his belly with the husks that the swine did eat". He realized that there was abundance in his father's house and returned to his father seeking forgiveness, and the father forgave him, and received him gladly. (cf.Luke15:16, 21 and 22). God receives His children when they return to Him in repentance.

In the Old Testament period God's anger burnt on the children of Israel, who worshipped idols, and committed sins; and He chastened them severely. David was no exception to such chastening when he committed sins. He was forgiven of his sins when he repented; nevertheless he reaped the consequences on this earth. He knew that he was going to be chastened, when he committed sins, and therefore, pleaded for mercy that He may lighten His chastisement.

In Psalm Chapter 6 David prays to God not rebuke him in His anger; neither chasten him in His displeasure. He pleads to God to lighten the severity of His chastisement.

David admitted before the LORD that he was weak, and that his bones were vexed, and his soul was vexed as well. His admittance depicts how much he humbled before the LORD. He questions God as to how long the LORD would keep away from him. He prays very earnestly to the LORD to return to him and deliver his soul. He asks God as to how he would remember the LORD, and give thanks to Him, from his grave, if he died because of chastisement.

David groaned in his spirit, with all the weakness in his body and soul, and says he cried whole night, virtually swimming in the bed soaked with his tears. His eyes became weak, because of his grief and he waxed old, because of all his enemies.

Nonetheless, David becomes self-confident very quickly, and consoles himself saying God heard his weeping and, therefore, commands the evil-doers and workers of iniquity to depart from his presence. He confidently says that the LORD heard his prayer and supplications. Then, he commands his enemies to return their base, and be ashamed, and sore vexed.

Indeed, the LORD does chasten His loved ones when they move away from His presence. He forgives the sins of His children, but He allows scars of the sin to remain in them. God will forget and does not remember our sins; but sinner's own conscience keeps him reminding him of his past sins. We must seek the Lord's help, when our past sins look upon us with contempt, because God never remembers our sin. It is Satan, who brings to our memory our past sins in order that we may fall again. The LORD chastens His children in order that they may not commit sins repeatedly.

Apostle Paul comes very heavily on those who repeatedly commit sins even after repenting of their sins with a decision to follow the Lord.

"Moreover the law entered, that the offence might abound. But where sin abounded, grace did much more abound" (Romans 5:20)

"What then? Shall we sin because we are not under the law but under grace? Certainly not!" (Romans 6:15).

CHAPTER 9
THE WISDOM FROM GOD

This message of cross is foolishness to the natural man but is wisdom to the one who accepts that Jesus died on the cross, was buried and God raised Him from the dead. There is power in that cross where Lord Jesus laid down His life for our sake.

For the message of the cross is foolishness to those who are perishing, but to us who are being saved it is the power of God (Acts 1:18).

To the Jew, who sought miracles and signs, and deliverance from the oppression of Roman Government, the message of cross was a stumbling block, and to the Gentiles, who sought philosophy, and salvation by their good works, the message of salvation was foolishness.

Not many of us were wise by human standards, and yet God chose the foolish things of this world to cause shame in wealthy and wise. God chose weak things of this world to put to shame the strong. God chose humble and hated things of this world to nullify the great and loved things of this world.

But the natural man receiveth not the things of the Spirit of God: for they are foolishness unto him: neither can he know them, because they are spiritually discerned. (1 Corinthians 2:14)

Natural man does not understand the spiritual things and everything about the cross and death of Jesus on the cross is a mere story for him; it is foolishness to him. He does not understand nor does he accept the truth. He cannot discern the spiritual things. Everything in the world and every fleshly pleasure appears to him as good and acceptable. But for those, who in obedience to the knowledge of the truth, the spiritual things are wisdom for him. The Lord gives them the wisdom to understand the cross and the benefits that flow from it. The power of the cross is understood by them because Holy Spirit gives them the wisdom to understand the sacrificial death of Lord Jesus on the cross.

SANCTIFICATION

It is by grace of God that we are saved, and not by our good works, and that no one can say that it is by one's good works that one is saved. No one would be able to boast in oneself because it is purely by the power of the cross that we are saved. It is because of the love of Lord Jesus Christ that we are in Him, who became wisdom for us from God. It is because of Him that we are made righteous and holy and redeemed from the bondage of sin.

Paul quotes from Old Testament a passage and says:

For it is written, I will destroy the wisdom of the wise, and will bring to nothing the understanding of the prudent. (1 Corinthians 1:19)

Many years ago Prophet Isaiah prophesied:

Therefore, behold, I will proceed to do a marvellous work among this people, even a marvellous work and a wonder: for the wisdom of their wise men shall perish, and the

*understanding of their prudent men shall be
hid. (Isaiah 29:14)*

Prophet Habakkuk prophesied that the
children of Israel, who were among the
heathen, would wonder marvelously at the
LORD's saying that He will work a work in their
days, which they will not believe even it was
told them. Very soon God raised Chaldeans to
attack Assyrians and destroyed city of Nineveh
beyond recognition to the utter dismay of the
children of Israel. (cf. Habakkuk 1:5).

In the early days of Christianity, the Gospel
was preached by the disciples of Jesus Christ,
first to the Jews, and then later to the Gentiles,
as we read in Acts Chapter 10, where we read
about Peter's preaching to the Gentile Roman
Centurion, and latter's conversion. Thereafter,
Paul and Barnabas were chosen by the Holy
Spirit to preach the Gospel.

Once when Apostle Paul was preaching and
travelling via the isle unto Paphos they saw a
sorcerer, a false prophet, who was a Jew and
his name was Barjesus. He was with the

SANCTIFICATION

Deputy of the country, Sergius Paulus, who was prudent man, desired to listen to Barnabas and Saul. But Barjesus, the sorcerer, whose name was interpreted as Elymas, became an obstacle to the Deputy and tried to turn him away from accepting Jesus as his Savior. Saul (who was called Paul) filled with the Holy Spirit, discerned the evil attitude, and mischief of Elymas. Paul said to him that he is full subtlety, mischief, the child of the devil, and the enemy of all righteousness, and because he never ceased to pervert the right ways of the Lord, he invoked the Lord's hand upon him and cursed him to be blind for a season. Immediately there fell on Elymas, a mist and darkness, and he went from Paul's presence seeking someone to lead him by hand. The Deputy saw the miracle, by which the sorcerer became blind for causing obstruction to the proclamation of the Gospel, and he believed the Lord (cf. Acts 13:6-12)

Paul preached the Gospel of Jesus Christ and narrated the history, even that of David, and they continued to despise his preaching. He asked them to believe in the Lord, and said

SANCTIFICATION

that the Lord will work a work through him, in their days, and they will not believe even though man declares it to them.

Behold, ye despisers, and wonder, and perish: for I work a work in your days, a work which ye shall in no wise believe, though a man declare it unto you. (Acts 13:41)

Those that boast may boast not in themselves but in the Lord.

That, according as it is written, He that glorieth, let him glory in the Lord. (1 Corinthians 1:31)

But let him that glorieth glory in this, that he understandeth and knoweth me, that I am the LORD which exercise lovingkindness, judgment, and righteousness, in the earth: for in these things I delight, saith the LORD. (Jeremiah 9:24)

CHAPTER 10
RIGHTOUESNESS

This is the second thing that Christ did for us by reconciling us with the Father in heaven.

"But of him are ye in Christ Jesus, who of God is made unto us wisdom, and righteousness, and sanctification, and redemption" (1 Corinthians 1:30)

Jesus was nor merely beaten up but He was scourged by Pilate, who little later, declared that He was innocent, yet ordered Him to be crucified. The whole trial was illegal.

Then Pilate therefore took Jesus, and scourged him. (John 19:1)

When the chief priests therefore and officers saw him, they cried out, saying, Crucify him, crucify him. Pilate saith unto them, Take ye him, and crucify him: for I find no fault in him. (John 19:6)

SANCTIFICATION

Lord Jesus was stripped upto a very humble state; and yet He was performing a very noble and pleasing deed on the cross. He offered his own body and blood for our sake and for the remission of our sins. God loved us so much so that He gave His only begotten son for this purpose. It pleased the Father to bruise Him on the cross. Woever believes in Him shall not perish but have everlasting life. It is not we who loved Him first but He loved us first.

"And they stripped him, and put on him a scarlet robe". (Matthew 27:28)

We are saved by an unmerited favor, called, Grace. It is the gift of God. When we could not stand right with God by our own good works, Christ died for us. By His death, in our stead, we are redeemed from Sin. Our righteousness is equivalent to filthy rags before God. Jesus purchased us with not with silver of God, but by His precious blood. We are His treasured possession.

"But we are all as an unclean thing, and all our righteousnesses are as filthy rags; and we all do fade as a leaf; and our iniquities, like the wind, have taken us away". (Isaiah 64:6)

Jesus was born as a Jew and God loved Israelites and called them as His People and the nation as His nation. The Bible asks us to pray for the peace of Jerusalem. We should pray for the peace of Jerusalem. Many Jews have accepted Jesus as their savior, but there are still many who reject Him as their Messiah. It would have been very good if all the Jews realized that Lord Jesus was divine, and fully human when He was on this earth and if they realized that He died for the sake of our sins. He was buried, rose from the dead and ascended into heaven. He is seated on the right hand of the Majesty. He comes back again as soon as all His enemies are brought to His footstool. Scriptures say that if they do not believe Jesus as their Messiah now, they will be brought to their knees to acknowledge Jesus as their Messiah during the period of "Great Tribulation".

That at the name of Jesus every knee should bow, of things in heaven, and things in earth,

and things under the earth; And that every
tongue should confess that Jesus Christ is
Lord, to the glory of God the Father.
(Philippians 2:10-11)

The very fact that their present day high
priests are not dying instantaneously for not
offering the bullock and a ram for themselves,
and the Lord's goat as sin offering and
confessing upon the live goat the sins of the
high priest and the sins of the people followed
by its letting loose into the wilderness itself
shows that they are in violation of the Mosaic
Law. (cf. Leviticus Chapter16)

The high priest starts by washing his flesh in
water and putting on linen garments. God
commanded to lay aside the beautiful priestly
garments of the high priest on this solemn
occasion wherein the high priest is seen in a
very humble stature, yet performing a very
noble and pleasing deed for the Lord, while
offering the sacrifices (Leviticus 16:4)

Jesus was without any sin and without any
blemish born of the Virgin Mary conceived of

SANCTIFICATION

the Holy Ghost (Matthew 1:20) and, therefore, he did not need any bullock for himself, but He became the Lamb of God and the sacrifice for our sake. John testified of him that He was the Lamb of God who takes away the sin.

The high priest takes a censer full of burning coals of fire from off the altar before the LORD, and his hands full of sweet incense beaten small, and brings it within the veil. He puts the incense upon the fire before the LORD, so that the cloud of the incense may cover the mercy seat that is upon the ark of the testimony; and if he failed to follow the said method his death was sure. The blood of the bullock is sprinkled with his finger upon the mercy seat eastward, and he sprinkles the blood before the mercy seat with his finger seven times. He goes back to the altar and kills the goat on which the lot fell as sin offering for the people and takes the blood of the goat within the veil and applies the blood and sprinkles just as he did with the blood of bullock for his own sake (Leviticus 16:15)

SANCTIFICATION

Jesus became the propitiation and substitution for our sake and fulfilled two-fold purpose of becoming sacrifice on behalf of us and bearing our sins upon himself as a substitute in our stead.

"Being justified freely by his grace through the redemption that is in Christ Jesus: Whom God hath set forth to be a propitiation through faith in his blood, to declare his righteousness for the remission of sins that are past, through the forbearance of God" (Romans 3:24–25)

Because the Tabernacle remained in the midst of the children of Israel with all their transgressions and uncleanness, Aaron, the high priest makes atonement for the holy place. He brings the live goat and lays both his hands upon the head of the live goat, signifying the transference of the sins of himself, and all the people of Israel on to the live goat, and confesses over the live goat all the iniquities of the children of Israel, and all the transgressions and all their sins, and sends it away by the hand of the fit man into the wilderness. The goat carries the iniquities of all the people of Israel unto a land not inhabited never to return again to the land where the children of Israel lived. The live goat on which the sins are confessed is led outside the camp by a fit man into the wilderness (Leviticus 16:16–19).

He, who lets the goat into the wilderness bathes his flesh in water and afterwards comes into the camp. Notice the shedding of the blood and its sprinkling covered their sins, yet the sins remained in the sanctuary until the high priest transferred the sins onto the live goat which carried the sins far into an uninhabited land. The letting of the scapegoat into the wilderness is after the high priest changes his garments of linen and puts on his priestly garments and offering of the fat of the sin offering to be burnt upon the altar (Leviticus 16:20–22)

"For he hath made him to be sin for us, who knew no sin; that we might be made the righteousness of God in him". (2 Corinthians 5:21)

JUSTIFICATION

1 Corinthians 1:30 But of him are ye in Christ Jesus, who of God is made unto us wisdom, and righteousness, and sanctification, and redemption

Justification is the declaration that our Lord and Savior Jesus Christ makes before the Father about a sinner, who believes in Jesus Christ and accepts him as his personal Savior. The sinner, who confesses him as the 'Lord' is justified by him as righteous because Christ has borne the sins of sinner on the cross of Calvary and made him righteous.

The justification originates in and through the grace. It is by grace through faith in him that a sinner is saved. No amount of good works can save a person, nor can justify him as righteous before God.

"Being justified freely by his grace through the redemption that is in Christ Jesus" Romans 3:24

SANCTIFICATION

It is judicial act that Jesus has performed on the cross. He paid the price for the redemption of sinner. He died in the stead of a sinner. That is how he justifies the sinner as righteous before the Father. All that a sinner needs to do is to accept the fact that Jesus Christ has died on the cross in his stead and rose from the dead on the third day.

It is by faith in Jesus as the redeemer that a sinner is saved and no charge is laid against him, irrespective of what gross sin he/she has committed. Every sin, except blasphemy of Holy Spirit, is pardonable by God. Christ has established the law by taking upon himself the penalty of sin, which is death.

As believers in Christ we have blessed hope that after death we will have a glorified bodies that are not made of hands but that which will be with the Lord eternally in the heavens. The body that we have now is made of dust and we groan in this body to be clothed to hide nakedness, in contrast to the glorified bodies that we will have in heaven.

SANCTIFICATION

Our bodies are made with the dust from this earth and, therefore, suffer sickness and decay in contrast to the glorified bodies that do not suffer any sickness or decay in eternity. This is the reason why we believers are happy to be absent in this body so that we can be present eternally with the Lord, and, therefore, we do not fear death. In this body we labor to earn for our life on this earth, but in eternity we are blessed with the rewards that our Lord gives us for the works that we have done for him on this earth.

Jesus died for our sake, and rose again from the dead giving us the blessed hope that even though we die we will rise once in glorified bodies.

"So also is the resurrection of the dead. It is sown in corruption ; it is raised in incorruption : (1 Corinthians 15 :42)

"Therefore if any man be in Christ, he is a new creature : old things are passed away ; behold, all things are become new ". (2 Corinthians 5 :17)

SANCTIFICATION

"The Price is already paid for" John 19:30

When Jesus therefore had received the vinegar, he said, It is finished: and he bowed his head, and gave up the ghost.

This is one of the seven sayings of Jesus when he was on the cross of Calvary. He was despised and rejected by man

This is the fulfillment of prophesy that is written in Isaiah 53 :4 -7 "Surely he hath borne our griefs, and carried our sorrows: yet we did esteem him stricken, smitten of God, and afflicted. But he was wounded for our transgressions; he was bruised for our iniquities: the chastisement of our peace was upon him; and with his stripes we are healed. All we like sheep have gone astray; we have turned every one to his own way ; and the LORD hath laid on him the iniquity of us all. He was oppressed, and he was afflicted, yet he opened not his mouth: he is brought as a lamb to the slaughter, and as a sheep before her shearers is dumb, so he openeth not his mouth ".

Leslie M. John   *Page 141*

SANCTIFICATION

He was led like a lamb to be slaughtered. His hands and feet were nailed. He was numbered with the transgressors his death.

Isaiah 53 :10 "Yet it pleased the LORD to bruise him; he hath put him to grief: when thou shalt make his soul an offering for sin, he shall see his seed, he shall prolong his days, and the pleasure of the LORD shall prosper in his hand. " His blood was paid as price for our redemption. There was nothing more, nor is anything more to be done any person for receiving salvation.

It is just the faith in him as Lord and Savior is the requirement to have everlasting life. Jesus took upon himself our infirmities and sin so that we may have everlasting life by accepting as our Lord. It pleased the Father to bruise him so that we may receive salvation. There is no price attached to that invaluable gift that is made available for us. The price is already paid.

Admonishing Galatians time and again, Apostle Paul continues to emphasize on the fact that there is salvation only in Jesus through faith by grace and not by law and works associated with it.

Getting entangled with law and with the thought that they need to do something to be saved, is tantamount to be under the yoke of bondage, he says. About, circumcision, he condemns it and says that if anyone is of the belief that circumcision is necessary for salvation or for justification, the obsession of such thought will not profit them and Christ and his blood is of nothing to them.

Everyone, who is circumcised becomes debtor to the whole law and Christ and his sacrifice has nothing for him. We are reckoned as righteous only by faith in Jesus and by his grace. Neither circumcision nor un-circumcision avails anything to a believer in Christ.

Walking in the Spirit and hatred of lust of the flesh are necessary on the part of a believer to lead a holy life. One great truth a believer has to understand is that flesh lusts against the

SANCTIFICATION

Spirit and the Spirit against the flesh and these are contrary to each other. If we are of the Spirit and are led by the Spirit we are not under the law and would not yield to the desires of the flesh.

After having known of the love of God through His one only begotten son, Jesus, why would we turn yet unto beggarly elements like observing the days, months, times and years, and be subject again to be under the bondage of the law? When the price for our sin and redemption is already paid for, why would we turn again to work for our salvation by ourselves? Salvation is available free of cost; the price is already paid for. All that is needed on the part of sinner is to believe that Jesus paid the price of his sin on the cross, and that he needs to believe in his/her heart this fact and accept him as his/her personal Savior.

Apostle Paul blesses those, who do not voluntarily subject themselves to be under the yoke of law, but accept Christ's death upon the cross. He says fulfilling the law of Christ is more important than that of the Old

SANCTIFICATION

Testament laws. No one should boast of himself nor glory himself/herself, but everyone should glorify Lord Jesus Christ, whose marks were borne by not only Apostle Paul but all those, who realize the efficacy of the blood of Lord Jesus Christ.

Paul's feels as if he was under the travail of child birth to explain to Galatians the difference between law and grace, and how hard it is to be under law rather than accept 'grace' alone as the way for salvation. He calls them, now, 'my little children', and try to explain to them about the implications in believing that law and works only would save them. Galatians were under the erroneous belief that law and works only can save them. They desired to take pride in a list of rules they prescribed for them and as they keep the rules they would consider them as perfect. That, in other words, renders a notion that man can earn his own salvation by keeping a set of rules, like being good and doing good etc.

SANCTIFICATION

These things help men to be good men but would not secure salvation that is available free of cost as a result of belief in the works of Jesus, the Son of God, did for men. He came down into this world to redeem us from the bondage of sin, and, therefore, took upon himself, our transgressions and died for our sake. The fruits of the Holy Spirit are love, joy, peace, longsuffering, gentleness, goodness, faith, Meekness, temperance. A saved man will have in him the Spirit of God and will have the fruits of the Holy Spirit.

However, possession of these good qualities without accepting Jesus as 'Lord' will not make us a man eligible to have eternal life. The only way to have eternal life is to believe in the efficacy of the blood of Jesus Christ and accept the fact that he died in our stead on the cross.

Paul explains to Galatians, just as a matured man explaining to children that all those who believe that law can save them are like those, who are of 'bondwoman' and all those who believe in the 'grace' of Jesus are like those, who are of free woman. He quotes from Old

SANCTIFICATION

Testament the things that have happened in *Abram*'s life as described in Genesis 16th Chapter.

Sarai sent her handmaid, Hagar to sleep with Abram, and a son was born. It was legalism on the part of *Sarai* and *Abram* a method that finds a way out for them. Later a son was born to **Abraham** and his wife **Sarah** as a consequence of the promise of God to them. This son of the promise of God was of faith in God and His grace.

The son, who was born to Hagar was of the flesh, and the son born of promise to Sarai, was blessed. The posterity of bondwoman are still under bondage of Mosaic law, and the posterity of the free woman, who are supposed to be free from the bondage of Mosaic law, have unfortunately, embraced the law and works as their way for salvation, rejected Messiah as their Savior, and are still under the bondage of law.

Paul desires that everyone should embrace the belief that it is by 'grace' of God that saves a man. Paul allegorizes this to the Jerusalem, which is above all, that consists of the posterity of Isaac, born of **Sarah** and that 'grace' alone saves a person. The legalists still insist that it is right to be under the law and keep the law to be saved. Such legalism will lead to the belief that there is no justification by the grace of God, but their own works will lead them to have eternal life.

Speaking of law and grace and the firm belief of Jews in their belief of laws plus works for their salvation rather than depending on pure mercy of God by grace through faith, another point that could we could meditate is on the fact as to why God did not have his own people, Jews, realize this so quickly that pure grace from God is alone sufficient for their salvation.

There is enough reason, as we understand, that God not only wanted his own people, Jews, to have their salvation, but also Gentiles to enjoy that privilege of calling him as 'Abba, Father'. .

SANCTIFICATION

Apostle Paul wonders if God cast away his people and immediately reaffirms that it was not so, because he was also of the seed of Abraham, of the tribe of Benjamin. God did not cast away his people, whom he foreknew. Even when Elias was taking pride in himself that he was alone available to intercede on behalf of Israel, God says to him, that he had reserved seven thousand men unto him, who could intercede on behalf of Israel. If the salvation, therefore, is by 'grace', then it is not by 'works'.

What then happened exactly that their attitude and belief has not changed yet? Yes, it is because God blinded their eyes and gave them spiritual slumber, that they should not see and that they may not have ears for hearing unto this day. Have Israel stumbled that they should fall then?

Apostle Paul himself answers these questions (Romans 11th Chapter) that God did not blind them or made them deaf because of they were stumbling blocks nor is it because they have stumbled, but because of the desire God had that everyone in the world, irrespective of Jews or Gentiles be saved and have eternal life.

Pillars are the strength of monuments and on the pillars are seen inscriptions or designs that either bring to us some remembrance of those, who responsibly raised them, or help us admire their beauty. Heaven does not need any pillar to support it, but the new Jerusalem, that John saw in his vision coming down from heaven was like a bride adorned for her bridegroom. In this New Jerusalem were seen the pillars on which were written the names of those, who served the living God, and the names of who those, who they served and represented. Some in the Church at Philadelphia (Rev 3:3-5) had not defiled their garments and they were worthy to receive blessings. God promised that he who overcomes shall walk with Him.

Those that overcome stand for the living God, and they are like pillars in the temple of God, and on them are written the names, such as 'name of my God', 'name of the city of my

SANCTIFICATION

God', which is 'new Jerusalem', and His new name. (Rev 21:2-5)

This is the difference between the earthly Jerusalem and the new Jerusalem that comes down from heaven. John saw a new heaven and a new earth after the first heaven and the first earth passed away and there was no more sea. In this new Jerusalem there was not seen any difference between Jews or Gentiles, but those who were there were all one in Christ. They had put on righteousness of Christ as their garments. They had received Jesus as their personal Savior and Lord by grace through faith in him.

More than anyone taking of airs of his belonging to any clan the important fact that is to be borne in mind is that it is the grace of God that saves a man. No man needs precious metals such as gold and silver to earn a place in new Jerusalem, but all that a man needs is to have simple faith in Jesus, the Son of God and make him Lord of his/her life. God wipes away their tears. There shall be no more death, no more sorrow, no more crying and no more pain. God shall give freely to all that thirst for such a life the fountain of life. He who overcomes the world and the temptations therein shall inherit the blessings from God and he shall be His son.

Apostle Paul explains elaborately the plan of God for the salvation of Gentiles in Romans 11th Chapter. It was not because Israel have stumbled nor because they were stumbling blocks to anybody that their eyes were blinded and their ears were short of hearing and understanding who their Messiah was and what exactly they needed to do for their salvation. They always insisted that because God had done something for them they owe to God something that they essentially do and such recompense only will fetch their salvation. It is because of their misunderstanding that salvation is come unto the Gentiles.

Paul warns Gentiles that they are like grafted wild olive tree in the places, where the branches of the natural branches were broken off. The Gentiles are partakers of the root and fatness of the natural olive tree. Therefore, he says, Gentiles should not be of high-minded, but fear. The branches of the natural olive tree were broken off by God himself, because of their unbelief, and the Gentiles, who were like wild olive trees have, now, the sap and blessings from the root of the natural olive tree. If Gentiles were to be high-minded and take pride in themselves or their own merits, God will not hesitate to chastise them. If God did not spare the natural branches of the olive tree would he tolerate the grafted olive tree; never!

In the book of Hosea the pathetic condition of Israel is seen. Israel, who had been blessed and to whom were the blessings and covenants given, continually fell from the presence of the Lord. In the sight of the Lord, who asked Hosea to marry a prostitute, Israel was similar to Prostitute, dishonest with her infidelity. God, who was like husband to them had to see her deviation from the honesty and loyalty, had to chastise them time and again. The Lord goes on to say that they are not his people, and he is not their God. He was like a frustrated husband trying to bring them to the path of salvation, yet they erred time and again. This was the reason, why God had to extend salvation to the Gentiles, thus making Jews and Gentiles one in Christ.

It was not a mystery that the Gentiles should be saved but one mystery was certainly there that God would form Church consisting of Jews and Gentiles, and that Church is above Jews and Gentiles. This purpose was hidden in God until it was revealed to us in Ephesians 2nd Chapter. The Church is the body of Christ. In this Church are no differences as to who is Jew and who is Gentile, but everyone has similar status. In this Church is seen no more distinction of earthly differences of race, ethnicity, clan, color, and nationality. It is the blood of Jesus that saves a man from being condemned to death and eternal destruction. It is the water that Jesus gives that becomes living water for the sinner. It is the life that Jesus gives to sinner that becomes eternal life.

God in his mercy and love for us quickened us in spirit together with Christ and by grace we are saved. He has given us the privilege to be seated together in heavenly places in Christ Jesus. Faith in him alone saved us and not of any good works in us or by us. If the salvation is by works, then anybody could boast of himself/herself by doing good works that he is worthy to receive salvation by himself, and of his good works. This renders the sacrifice of Jesus of null effect. The very purpose of Jesus coming into this world was to bear on himself, the sins of the world so that whoever believes in him could be saved. If good works of any man could save him, then Christ need not have come to this world. There is a fundamental error in believing that good works of any man would save him from his sins. "We are his workmanship, created in Christ Jesus unto good works".

This was in the plan of God even before the foundation of the world. The good works of a man will not save him but in Christ Jesus we will do good works as a result of having the fruit of the Holy Spirit. "We were without Christ, and aliens from the commonwealth of

SANCTIFICATION

Israel" We had no hope of having salvation but in the blood of Jesus Christ we are made one.

Apostle Paul emphasizes in Romans 6th chapter that sin shall not have dominion over a born-again child because he/she is not under the law, but under grace. Those who seek to do good works and earn salvation by their own works have nullified the importance of blood of Jesus Christ and in their lives the blood of Jesus Christ that cleanses the sin has no value for them. They diligently keep doing good works neglecting the repeated emphasis from the Lord Jesus Christ that his blood saves and gives eternal life to all those, who go to him and accept him as the Lord.

After having been delivered from the bondage of sin by grace through faith should a child of God keep sinning because he is under the grace but not under law? Paul very firmly says, "God forbid". Never should a child of God return to sin and lose blessings from God. Salvation is not lost for those who are saved in the blood of Jesus Christ\; however, the Scripture does not endorse repeated sinning.

SANCTIFICATION

God will surely chide and chastise the one that falls repeatedly into sin and seeks grace time and again.

Should we not consider the fact that if he yield to sin we are servants to sin and sin becomes our master; we are under grace and we should remain servants to our Lord and be of obedience to righteousness. We were, once, servants of sin, but after accepting Jesus as our master, we have become servants of righteousness. We have our fruit unto holiness, and everlasting life. The law has concluded all of us under sin, but the gift of God is eternal life through Lord Jesus Christ.

John Chapter 10 deals with the subject of the relationship between him and those who have accepted him as the Lord. The comparison of the shepherd and his flock with Jesus his beloved ones is that Jesus is good shepherd. He is the door and there is no other way to the pasture. A thief does not enter the sheepfold by the door, but enters climbing the wall and entering some other way. Jesus said, if any man enters by Him he shall be saved. A good shepherd gives life for his flock, but a hireling does not give his life. Hireling would run away leaving sheep helpless, when he encounters some danger.

On the contrary, a good shepherd will leave ninety nine sheep aside and seek after the lost one sheep, and finds it and brings it back to the flock. Jesus is our good shepherd. 'I am the good shepherd, and know my sheep, and am known of mine '. The word, 'know ' here shows the love that the sheep show toward their good shepherd, whom they trust and obey. Jesus asserts here that he is the good shepherd, who will not let his sheep be stolen by his enemy. He would leave ninety nine sheep aside for some time to go in search of one lost or backslidden sheep to bring it back to join the ninety nine.

John 10:27-30 'My sheep hear my voice, and I know them, and they follow me: And I give unto them eternal life; and they shall never perish, neither shall any man pluck them out of my hand. My Father, which gave them me, is greater than all; and no man is able to pluck them out of my Father's hand. I and my Father are one. John 10:14 'I am the good shepherd, and know my sheep, and am known of mine '.

The word, 'know ' here shows the love that the sheep show toward their good shepherd, whom they trust and obey. Jesus asserts here that he is the good shepherd, who will not let his sheep be stolen by his enemy. He would leave ninety nine sheep aside for some time to go in search of one lost or backslidden sheep to bring it back to join the ninety nine. John 10:27-30 'My sheep hear my voice, and I know them, and they follow me: And I give unto them eternal life; and they shall never perish, neither shall any man pluck them out of my hand. My Father, which gave them me, is greater than all; and no man is able to pluck them out of my Father's hand. I and my Father are one. John 10:14'

Jesus Christ is the Son of God and very God Himself. Jesus said, in John 10:30 'I and my Father are one '. He said in John 16:15 'All things that the Father hath are mine: therefore said I, that he shall take of mine, and shall shew it unto you '. He said in John 17:11 'And now I am no more in the world, but these are in the world, and I come to thee. Holy Father, keep through thine own name those whom thou hast given me, that they may be one, as we are '. Apostle Paul wrote about Jesus Christ in Colossians 1:15-18 'Who is the image of the invisible God, the firstborn of every creature: For by him were all things created, that are in heaven, and that are in earth, visible and invisible, whether they be thrones, or dominions, or principalities, or powers: all things were created by him, and for him: And he is before all things, and by him all things consist. And he is the head of the body, the church: who is the beginning, the firstborn from the dead; that in all things he might have the preeminence.

When we think of the sin King David did by committing adultery with Bathsheba we cannot think of any reason why God would not forgive our sins. David was blessed one, God chose him to be King, yet one day when [2Sam 11th Chapter] saw from the roof of his home, a beautiful woman named Bathsheba washing herself. David sent messengers and took her, and committed sin with her. He did not end his iniquity there but conspired and got her husband, Uriah, killed in the battle. God punished David for his sin. David's son from Bathsheba died, and David had to pay great penalty for his sin. Yet, when David repented of his sin, He had compassion on him and forgave him, and restored him.

Jesus became poor for us even though he was rich in his glory and was with the Father from eternity. He said he is the beginning and he is the end; he is the Alpha and Omega. He is the creator of this universe, he owns everything, every creation and he is the King of kings, he is the Lord or lords, and he is the God of gods.

Lord Jesus was in the form of God and did not think it robbery to be to equal with God, but made himself of no repute, took the form of servant, and became like a man and dwelt among us. He was born of the Virgin Mary, by the works of Holy Spirit, and was laid in a manger. He was raised in a poor family. His earthly parents offered turtle doves as

SANCTIFICATION

offerings (Luke 2:24), which was a provision
made for poor and those, who could not offer
bull or goat as sacrifice as per Old Testament
Law. In Colossians 1st Chapter verses 15 to
17, there is a clear description that Jesus the
creator. He is the image of the invisible God,
the first born of every creature, and by him
were all things created; yet we see that he took
the form of man for our sake. He testified, in
Luke 9:58 how poor he was on this earth.

All this was took place because Jesus became a
sacrifice on our behalf, when he took upon
himself, our curse, our sin and shed his
precious blood upon the cross of Calvary. The
salvation is received by his 'grace' through
faith in him that he died and rose for our sake,
and by accepting his as 'Lord '. He offered
himself on the cross so that we may have
riches in him. The earthly riches are not true
riches. What if a man earns whole earth his
soul? We are saved by his precious blood and
not of any of our works. We are not purchased
by gold and/or silver, but by the blood of
Jesus, who paid it as price for our salvation.

CHAPTER 11
POSITIONAL SANCTIFICATION

'Sanctification' differs from 'Justification', insomuch that justification is the legal action by which the man accused of charges is acquitted, and justified as 'not guilty'. After a person is declared as 'not guilty' the person is free from accusations and will not be punished, for any of the crimes he might or might not have committed. The verdict 'not guilty' is powerful enough to set free the accused from all charges, and from the time he is declared 'not guilty' he is innocent of all the charges leveled against him. The person is set free and he can mingle with the society in a normal way as does any other citizen.

Sanctification, on the other hand, is not achieved in one stage but in several stages. It can be divided mainly into three stages and they are:

1. Positional sanctification _

Leslie M. John   *Page 163*

SANCTIFICATION

2. Practical sanctification/Progressive Sanctification
3. Perfect sanctification

Positional sanctification is achieved when a man accepts Jesus as His personal savior by confessing his sins to Him, and believes in heart that God raised Him from the dead. This is the Spiritual birth, that is to say, the man is born from above. Every man is born into this world, physically, once from his parents. The man is said to be 'born-again', when he is born from above, and unless a man is born-again he cannot see the kingdom of God.

Jesus answered and said unto him, Verily, verily, I say unto thee, Except a man be born again, he cannot see the kingdom of God. (John 3:3)

Holy Spirit takes residence in his heart and indwells him immediately when He is born-again. There is no separate waiting period required for Holy Spirit to come and take residence in a believer's heart. This is one time action and will not be repeated. We need filling up of Holy Spirit, time and again, at different

periods of time, when we venture a new task
for the Lord.

Jesus healed the impotent man, who was lying
at Bethesda pool, for thirty eight years. The
man totally depended on Jesus for healing by
saying that "Sir, I have no man, when the water
is troubled, to put me into the pool", in an
answer to the question from Jesus, who asked
him, "Wilt thou be made whole?" Jesus said to
him to take up his bed and walk.

*Jesus saith unto him, Rise, take up thy bed,
and walk. (John 5:8)*

Afterward when Jesus saw him in the temple
He said to the man "Behold, thou art made
whole: sin no more, lest a worse thing come
unto thee" (cf. John 5:7-14)

In another occasion, when the scribes and
Pharisees brought to Jesus, a woman caught
red-handed in adultery, and demanded that
she be stoned to death, according to Mosaic
Law, He said to them "He that is without sin
among you, let him first cast a stone at her".
They all were convicted by their own

Leslie M. John   *Page 165*

conscience, and "went out one by one, beginning at the eldest even unto the last". Then Jesus lifted Himself and asked her if anyone condemned her. The woman addressing Jesus as "Lord" said, "No man, Lord". Then Jesus set her free from her sin and said to her not to sin any more. (cf. John 8:2–11)

"She said, No man, Lord. And Jesus said unto her, Neither do I condemn thee: go, and sin no more" (John 8:11)

Earlier in another occasion scribes blamed Jesus saying that He was blaspheming God by forgiving sins, by His own authority, but then Jesus said to them that the 'Son of man" had the power on earth to forgive sins.

But that ye may know that the Son of man hath power on earth to forgive sins, (then saith he to the sick of the palsy,) Arise, take up thy bed, and go unto thine house. (Matthew 9:6)

Lord Jesus Christ is the Savior and salvation belongs to Him. There no salvation in any another.

Leslie M. John   *Page 166*

SANCTIFICATION

Neither is there salvation in any other: for there is none other name under heaven given among men, whereby we must be saved. (Acts 4:12)

We are consecrated to be holy till we die. We are saved from our sins and punishment. Our sins are cleaned in the precious blood of Lord Jesus Christ, who purchased us not with silver and gold but by His own blood. We are not supposed to sin after we are born-again.

CHAPTER 12
PROGRESSIVE SANCTIFICATION

Progressive sanctification is that in which a believer is purified every moment and every day in his life. It could be called Practical sanctification also.

There were Ten Commandments given to the children of Israel and many other commandments associated with them as described in Exodus, Leviticus, Numbers and Deuteronomy. In Genesis there were commandments given, however, they were all verbal.

Until the Law was given the guilt was not imputed to the man as Sin. However, God did not leave Adam and Eve to go unpunished from their transgression of God's verbal commandment. Likewise, He did not leave Cain to go unpunished for killing his brother, Abel. After that God punished the whole world by flood, during Noah's period, except Noah's family and the livestock according as God

SANCTIFICATION

wished, because of the wickedness in the world. Later, God punished Sodom and Gomorrah with fire and brimstone.

Man failed to keep the Ten Commandments and no one could be justified under Mosaic Law. God spoke through prophets, and then lastly through His one and only Son, Jesus Christ.

All power is given to the Lord Jesus Christ, and He has the keys to the hell and hades. He is authorized to forgive sins of any man, who confesses his sin to Him and accepts Him as Savior, and believes in heart that God raised Him from the dead. There is no savior except Jesus Christ.

Jesus came in the form of servant and in the likeness of man, and took upon Himself the iniquity of man and died on the cross; he was buried and his body did not decompose, or get corrupted. He rose from the dead with glorified body; a body that could pass the closed door of house; a body that could appear and disappear at His will; a body that could travel from place to place instantaneously; and a body that could eat fish.

God's desire was that you and I are conformed to the image of His Son. It is God's desire that we live a perfect sinless life after we have received salvation. He offered His one and only Son, Jesus Christ, who was the "Lamb of God", to die in our stead. Jesus bore our sins and died a sacrificial death on behalf of us.

Jesus did not say that we should not follow the commandments; rather He placed us on a higher level. He overcame the world and He wants us to overcome the world. He came to fulfill the law and He fulfilled it.

Think not that I am come to destroy the law, or the prophets: I am not come to destroy, but to fulfil. (Matthew 5:17)

Some of the commandments Jesus gave, to His disciples, on the Mount of Olives are as follows:

SANCTIFICATION

Ye have heard that it was said by them of old time, Thou shalt not commit adultery: But I say unto you, That whosoever looketh on a woman to lust after her hath committed adultery with her already in his heart. (Matthew 5:27-28)

But I say unto you, That whosoever shall put away his wife, saving for the cause of fornication, causeth her to commit adultery: and whosoever shall marry her that is divorced committeth adultery. (Matthew 5:32)

But I say unto you, Love your enemies, bless them that curse you, do good to them that hate you, and pray for them which despitefully use you, and persecute you; (Matthew 5:44)

There are many more as we read in Matthew Chapters 5 to 7. These are not as much applicable to every believer as they were applicable to His disciples. Jesus was declaring to His disciples the "kingdom of heaven", and the characteristics of the kingdom. He was also telling them how blessed are those who follow His doctrines.

SANCTIFICATION

When Jesus saw the multitudes He went up into a mountain and sat down, and when His disciples came to Him, he taught them these beatitudes, also called the "blessings". It does not mean that he avoided teaching multitudes who followed Him. Christians would struggle to understand and keep the message of these beatitudes, if they are taken literally as belonging to them, primarily because they were not addressed to the Church, but to the disciples and about the "kingdom of heaven".

And seeing the multitudes, he went up into a mountain: and when he was set, his disciples came unto him: (Matthew 5:1)

And if thy right eye offend thee, pluck it out, and cast it from thee: for it is profitable for thee that one of thy members should perish, and not that thy whole body should be cast into hell. (Matthew 5:29)

When we read those commandments it would seem impossible to keep them on daily basis. Jesus gave concise summary of all the commandments in just three verses.

SANCTIFICATION

Jesus said unto him, Thou shalt love the Lord thy God with all thy heart, and with all thy soul, and with all thy mind. This is the first and great commandment. And the second is like unto it, Thou shalt love thy neighbour as thyself. On these two commandments hang all the law and the prophets. (Matthew 22:37-40)

However, human as we are, and living in this world with compelling demands at various places, and in various situations, we fail to keep the commandments of the Lord, time and again. That failure leaves us to be at the mercy of our savior Lord Jesus Christ, whenever we falter.

Our primary goal, after being saved, should be to count ourselves as dead to sin and alive to God through Lord Jesus Christ. It is possible because we depend on God and do not allow sin to have dominion over us, because we are not under the law, but under grace.

Apostle Paul wrote

For ye know what commandments we gave you by the Lord Jesus. For this is the will of God,

SANCTIFICATION

even your sanctification, that ye should abstain from fornication: That every one of you should know how to possess his vessel in sanctification and honour; (1 Thessalonians 4:2-4)

We thank God because we are not servants of sin, but obeyed the Lord that we will follow Him and His teachings. Because we are freed from sin by the blood of Lord Jesus Christ we became the servants of righteousness. Earlier we were servants of the Devil and his ploys, but now we are servants of righteousness (cf. Romans 6:11, Romans 6:14, Romans 6:17-18)

After having been saved an individual needs continual sanctification to be conformed to the image of Christ. This is the aim and desire of God that we all, who are saved by the precious blood of Jesus Christ, become like Christ. The Bible promises all those, who are saved, that they will become partakers of divine nature.

Whereby are given unto us exceeding great and precious promises: that by these ye might be partakers of the divine nature, having

SANCTIFICATION

*escaped the corruption that is in the world
through lust. (2 Peter 1:4)*

Apostle Paul wrote in Romans 8:29-30 and
Ephesians 1:5, 11 for the edification of
believers in Christ and the Scriptures give us
great hope of being confirmed to the Son of
God, Lord Jesus Christ, but this is yet future.
The prophecies are written in past tense, and
many of them are fulfilled, and many of them
are yet to be fulfilled. The hope given to the
believers in Christ that they will be confirmed
to the image of His Son is yet to be fulfilled

*"For whom he did foreknow, he also did
predestinate to be conformed to the image of
his Son, that he might be the firstborn among
many brethren. Moreover whom he did
predestinate, them he also called: and whom
he called, them he also justified: and whom he
justified, them he also glorified". (Romans
8:29-30)*

God said as many as are led by the Spirit of
God, they are the sons of God, and the sons of
God have not received the spirit of bondage

Leslie M. John   *Page 175*

again to fear, but received the spirit of adoption. This privilege entails us to call God as "Abba, Father" and the Spirit bears witness that we are the children of God. (cf. Romans 8:14–16).

Apostle Paul explains that the heir as long as he is a child does not differ from a servant because even though he is the lord of all, he is under tutor and governors until the time appointed of the father. The children are still considered as in bondage under the elements of the world.

When the fullness of time was come God sent His one and only begotten Son, born of the virgin Mary, conceived of the Holy Ghost, made under law, to redeem that was under the law that we might receive the adoption of sons. Therefore, we are no more servants but sons and daughters, and if it is so, then we are heirs of God through Christ.

Lord Jesus Christ redeemed us from the bondage of Mosaic Law and gave us the liberty to be under the provisions of Gospel to gain the privilege of being the adopted sons and receive the full benefits promised to the children of Israel.

Even though the promises, covenants and law belonged to the children of Israel, yet, now those who accept Lord Jesus Christ as savior are set free from the stringent Laws of Moses. Our salvation is by grace through faith. (Galatians 4:1–7).

It was according to God's good pleasure of His will that Gentiles are also made equal partners of the inheritance of heavenly blessings. Now, therefore, in this dispensation there is no difference between Jew and Gentile. A Jew has to come to the Lord Jesus Christ just as any Gentile would come and accept Him as the Savior.

Jesus is the only way, the Truth, and the Life and no one can come to the Father except through Him. If Jews need heavenly blessings and are desirous of being conformed, in future, to the image of Lord Jesus Christ, who relinquished His glory when He came into this world as a servant in the form of man, was crucified, died, buried and rose from the dead with uncorrupted body, in his glorified body, ascended into heaven, and seated on the right hand of the Majesty, then they necessarily have to accept Lord Jesus Christ as their Messiah. If they continue to be in rebellion of the Gospel of Jesus Christ, then, according to the word of God, they lose the privilege of being conformed to the image of His Son in eternity.

"Having predestinated us unto the adoption of children by Jesus Christ to himself, according to the good pleasure of his will" (Ephesians 1:5)

"In whom also we have obtained an inheritance, being predestinated according to the purpose of him who worketh all things after the counsel of his own will" (Ephesians 1:11)

God predestines us unto the adoption as children by Lord Jesus Christ to Himself according to the good pleasure of His will. In

SANCTIFICATION

Him we have obtained an inheritance according to the purpose of Him. The very first assertion the scripture makes here is that God foreknew those who would be conformed to the image of his Son, Lord Jesus Christ. Therefore, God predestined those who, in his foreknowledge, would respond to His call and accept Lord Jesus Christ as their savior. Those, who respond and confess their sins to Lord Jesus Christ, will be forgiven of their sins and justified.

They are assured of being confirmed, in future, to the image of his son and, therefore, He called them and will glorify them in eternity. Surely God foreknew those who would be conformed to the image of his Son. Therefore, he called them and justified and glorified them. None of these assertions add emphasis to imaginations that God predestined some to hell or God forcibly converts any human to his side.

The Bible contains message of Gospel of Jesus Christ and the message is that Lord Jesus Christ is the Savior, that He is the Son of God, that He and the Father are one, and that there is no salvation outside of Him. Jesus is the way, the truth and the light.

"And not only they, but ourselves also, which have the firstfruits of the Spirit, even we ourselves groan within ourselves, waiting for the adoption, to wit, the redemption of our body" (Romans 8:23)

"Who are Israelites; to whom pertaineth the adoption, and the glory, and the covenants, and the giving of the law, and the service of God, and the promises" (Romans 9:4)

"To redeem them that were under the law, that we might receive the adoption of sons" (Galatians 4:5)

It was God's good pleasure that according to His will he predestined us unto adoption of children by Jesus Christ. Man has no free will to do anything against the will of God to be predestined either to become the child of God or to go against God.

SANCTIFICATION

It is God who controls men's will. Man can, by himself, do nothing other than choosing for himself eternal damnation by rejecting Jesus as Savior. There is difference between choice a man makes and the will that he has. Men's will is not free to make any decision against God's will, but men can make their choices. The will of men cannot overpower God's will.

The will of God is all powerful and God makes the world to move according to His will, and yet he provides a choice and chance for man to repent of his sin, and choose the living God. Jehovah is living God and not an idol. Idols do not move, do not speak, and do not do anything on their own.

Jehovah is the living God who loved us and gave His one and only begotten Son to be crucified for our sake in order that we might be saved from perishing. Whosoever believes in Jesus as Savior will not perish but will have everlasting life.

There is inheritance promised to those who believe in Lord Jesus Christ as Savior and we are predestinated to have that inheritance in future and to be conformed to the image of His Son. This is according to the purpose of Him who works all things according to the counsel of His own will. Jehovah does not need our counsel; and His counsel and His purposes are final.

The image of God is lost in the Garden of Eden when man committed transgression against the will of God and sinned against God's law. God is the creator and man is under His will and His purposes, yet man has the choice to choose the better or worse.

The first man exercised his choice in a bad way and lost the image of God. In His mercy God desires to restore that lost image to all those who have sinned. Bible says there is no one righteous; not even one and every one has come short of the glory of God. If we say that we have not sinned, then we make God a liar. The only way to get out of that bad situation and to be conformed to the image of the Son, Lord Jesus Christ, is to repent of sins and turn to God and accept that Lord Jesus Christ is the only Savior.

To be conformed to the image of Christ is a life-time process and we are continually being "changed into the same image from glory to glory, even by the Spirit of the Lord". Paul confirms that he had not attained perfectness in his lifetime, and yet continued to work towards being perfect. The Bible admonishes us that we should put off anger, wrath, malice, blasphemy, filthy communication out of our mouths, and do not tell lies one to another. It is obvious that we fail in one of these many times, and, therefore, we need to be purified. Even though we become a new creature in Christ, we who are fallible humans; need to be renewed of the spirit, and knowledge of the image of the Lord. (cf. *2 Corinthians 3:18, Colossians 3:8-10*)

That I may know him, and the power of his resurrection, and the fellowship of his sufferings, being made conformable unto his death; If by any means I might attain unto the resurrection of the dead. Not as though I had

SANCTIFICATION

*already attained, either were already perfect:
but I follow after, if that I may apprehend that
for which also I am apprehended of Christ
Jesus. (Philippians 3:10–12)*

CHAPTER 13
PERFECT SANCTIFICATION

*And there shall in no wise enter into it any
thing that defileth, neither whatsoever worketh
abomination, or maketh a lie: but they which
are written in the Lamb's book of life.
(Revelation 21:27)*

Heaven is the throne of God, who is holy and
holy as He is, nothing that is impure or unholy
will enter His abode. Nothing that works
abomination, or defiles the abode of God will
see the kingdom of heaven. It is a place
reserved for those whose names are written in
the "Lamb's book of Life".   Our citizenship is
in heaven and we look for our savior, Lord
Jesus Christ, who will change our wicked and
sinful bodies into glorious bodies worthy of
entering into His presence. This perfection is
achieved only when the Lord returns again.

It is not possible for anyone on this earth to
attain perfection as long as one is in the
wicked fleshly body made of dust. However,

that should not be an excuse for any believer to be discouraged and be drifted away from the path of righteousness, which God wants us to tread on. The more negligent we are towards to God the more we drift away from Him rendering ourselves to chastisement. Believer will not lose salvation but will surely be chastised for his repeated sins. If we confess our sins, then He is faithful to forgive our sins.

We know that every one begotten of God does not sin, but he that has been begotten of God keeps himself, and the wicked one does not touch him. (1 John 5:18)

There is no temptation that is beyond our capacity to endure and overcome it; rather in every situation when we are tempted by the devil, God provides a way for us to escape from it. It is by our choice that we deliberately fall into sin. God never tempts man; rather He always helps man to overcome temptation.

For our conversation is in heaven; from whence also we look for the Saviour, the Lord

Jesus Christ: Who shall change our vile body, that it may be fashioned like unto his glorious body, according to the working whereby he is able even to subdue all things unto himself. (Philippians 3:20-21)

BODY, SOUL AND SPIRIT

Perfect sanctification is complete only when body and soul of a person are purified fully to the extent that there is no blemish in any one of them. This perfection is achieved only when Lord Jesus Christ returns again to receive all those who are saved. The body is not redeemed until it is buried in the grave and resurrected.

While those who were saved in Christ before He comes again will rise from the dead, those who are alive will be caught up to meet the Lord in the air to be with Him for ever and ever. They will reign, along with Jesus, over those who were in the 'kingdom of heaven'.

The **body** is made of dust, which is also called as 'flesh' by Paul, will project the consequences of man's sin. It will return to earth as dust at death. The body of saved one will rise in glory. The **soul** is the inner man (the very man – ask yourself who you are!) The soul of man, who is saved, is sealed by the Holy Spirit unto everlasting life. The soul of unsaved man will be cast into 'lake of fire'. The **spirit** that God blew in to the nostrils of man returns to God. (In some passages of the scripture 'spirit' is used to refer soul)

THE TRIUNE GOD

Unless triune God involves in purifying body and soul perfect sanctification of man is not achieved. In the perfect sanctification of man the work of Triune God is clearly seen.

In the beginning was the Word, and the Word was with God, and the Word was God. (John 1:1)

The word became flesh and dwelt among us. John bare witness of Lord Jesus Christ, saying He was the one of whom He spoke, that would come after him. Jesus was before John and even before Abraham.

Jesus said unto them, Verily, verily, I say unto you, Before Abraham was, I am. (John 8:58)

John was the forerunner of Jesus and cried in the wilderness "Prepare ye the way of the Lord, make his paths straight" and baptized and preached the baptism of repentance for the remission of sins. He bore witness of Jesus, who was to come after Him, yet He was preferred before him, because Jesus was before him.

Next day when he saw Jesus he said "*Behold the Lamb of God, who takes away the sin of the world*". John said Jesus was the One, who will baptize with the Holy Ghost. He saw the "*Spirit descending from heaven like a dove, and it abode upon him*". *(cf. John 1:32-34)*

As we read in Luke chapter 4:1 when Jesus being fully of the Holy Spirit returned from River Jordan, and was led by the Spirit into the wilderness, where He fasted for forty days and forty nights. The devil tempted Him and He overcame all the temptations, thus defeating the devil, before He started His ministry on the earth.

After Jesus had started His ministry He said on day to His disciples that He will pray to the Father, who will send unto them "another Comforter", who will abide with us, as also with the disciples. Hinting at His death, burial and Resurrection Jesus said that it is expedient that He should go away to the Father in order that the Holy Spirit, the Comforter, may come.

Confusing as it may seem to them who lack wisdom from heaven, the triune God is totally out of their understanding (cf. John 14:16, 15:26, John 16:7, Genesis 1:2, Genesis 1:26, Genesis 11:7, John 1:1, John 1:14, John 10:30 etc.)

Lord Jesus Christ overcame death when God raised Him from the dead on the third day. One important point that we always should bear in mind that the Father and the Son are one, even though we find in scriptures, several times, as God raised the Son from the dead. (cf. Acts 2:24, 3:26, 10:40, Romans 10:9).

Much confusion prevails in the minds of believers as in those, who confront Christians by saying that Jesus is the "Son of God" and not God. It is all because they have feeble and frail knowledge of the Father, the Son and the Holy Spirit.

Jesus said:

I and my Father are one. (John 10:30)

The Father causes an effect in us to realize the truth of the knowledge of the Triune God, and leaves the choice for us to accept His one and only begotten Son, as the Savior.

Holy Spirit takes residence in the hearts of those who accept the 'Son of God' as their savior. Neither the Father nor the Son, or the Holy Spirit puts any pressure or compels anyone or forcibly converts anyone to follow God. Holy Spirit guides us, convicts us of our sins, and leads us to the path of righteousness. Jesus had already paid the price

SANCTIFICATION

of our salvation, and when this realization comes into the heart of man, he will accept Jesus as the Lord, and confesses his sins to Him, and believes in heart that God raised the Son from the dead. Salvation is the work of the Triune God (Cf. Philippians 2:13, 1 Corinthians 6:11, 2 Thessalonians 2:13, 1 Peter 1:2, Galatians 5:22-23)

If anyone rejects the Jesus as the Lord, after having received the knowledge of the truth, then there remains no more sacrifice for sins. If a person continues to be in sin and chooses to reject Jesus, then God hands him over to his vile desires. The consequence of rejecting Jesus as the Lord is very serious. He/she stands condemned of his/her sins at the 'great white throne' judgment and will be cast into 'lake of fire', which is second death.

For if we sin wilfully after that we have received the knowledge of the truth, there remaineth no more sacrifice for sins, (Hebrews 10:26)

For this cause God gave them up unto vile affections: for even their women did change the natural use into that which is against nature: (Romans 1:26)

THE POWER OF DEATH

God commanded the man saying to him that he may freely eat of every tree of the garden but shall not eat of the tree of the knowledge of good and evil. The wages of transgression of God's command was that he shall surely die in the day he eats thereof. (Genesis 2:16–17).

God made woman out of one of the ribs of man and the woman became man's wife. Adam and Eve lived happily until sin entered their lives through the deception by serpent, who enticed Eve to eat from the forbidden tree.

The lust of the flesh, the lust of the eyes, and the pride of life, with desires of satisfying her body in her way, to satisfy her eyes, the thing that looked pleasant to her eyes, and the pursuit of earthly knowledge made her to yield to the temptation of Satan. She not only ate the fruit from the forbidden tree, but she gave it to man, who also ate of it, and thus they became enemies to God.

Adam and Eve heard the voice of Jehovah Elohim, when He was walking in the garden in the cool of the day. They were afraid and hid themselves from His presence.

When God called Adam he answered saying he hid from the LORD because he was naked; and, thereafter, he and Eve started blame game. Adam blamed Eve for his transgression, and Eve blamed the serpent for her transgression.

Then, God cursed serpent to be loathsome creature among all the creatures and will crawl on its belly throughout its life.

The ground was cursed for man and God said that he should sweat and toil to plow the land, which will produce thorns and thistles also, along with good crops.

SANCTIFICATION

God said to the woman that she will bear children in travail and her husband will be her desire, and he will rule over her.

However, God made for Adam and Eve coats of skin, and clothed them, signifying that they were reconciled to Him according to His mercy. (Genesis 3:1–21).

It was when Adam and Eve sinned that Satan gained power over death and death remained in his domain. It is evident from the words of Jesus that Satan has his own kingdom and demons are as his followers. (Cf. Matthew 12:24-27)

"Whosoever committeth sin transgresseth also the law: for sin is the transgression of the law". (1 John 3:4)

The transgression of law is sin. Does it mean that it is applicable only from the time Mosaic Law was given? No. God's law prevailed even before the written law was given. Man was governed under Conscience and God punished sin even before the written law was given. The death reigned from Adam to Moses even when there was no written law, and death continued to have its power on sinner.

THE STING OF DEATH

"O death, where is thy sting? O grave, where is thy victory?" (1 Corinthians 15:55)

GOSPEL OF JESUS CHRIST

Gospel means good news. Gospel of Jesus Christ means the gospel of His death, burial and resurrection. He died on the cross, for our sake and on behalf of us, bearing our sin upon Him, in order that we may be delivered from our sin, and that we may receive everlasting life.

The salvation is available for everyone, irrespective of Jew or Gentile, who confesses Jesus as the Lord, and believes in heart that God raised Him from the dead. It deals with confession of sins to Jesus, and the salvation by grace through faith. This is the salvation of mankind that Apostle Paul spoke of as the "Grace of God". Those who accept Jesus as personal savior will be saved and justified as 'not guilty' of any sin.

EVERLASTING GOSPEL

Everlasting Gospel is preached to those at the end of 'great tribulation' until the judgment of nations begins. It differs from the 'Gospel of kingdom' and 'Gospel of Grace". The everlasting Gospel is preached to those who did not believe in Jesus before the Church is caught up to be with Him for ever and ever.

There is no second chance for repent of sins after Jesus comes again; however for those who are left behind the message of kingdom of God is preached by two witnesses.

All those who call upon God accepting Jesus as their Messiah, will enter into His kingdom that lasts for a thousand years. Those who reject Jesus as Messiah will pass though 'great tribulation' to be judged and to them is 'everlasting gospel' preached.

It is not a salvation message but this message contains two facts. One is that of the victory of those of meeting the Lord in the air, and that of those who have entered into 'thousand-year-reign' of Jesus Christ, and the second is of judgment is proclaimed by the angel. (Cf. Re 7:9–14; Lu 21:28; Ps 96:11–13; Isa 35:4–10)

"And I said unto him, Sir, thou knowest. And he said to me, These are they which came out of great tribulation, and have washed their robes, and made them white in the blood of the Lamb". (Revelation 7:14)

Let the heavens rejoice, and let the earth be glad; let the sea roar, and the fulness thereof; Let the field exult and all that is therein. Then shall all the trees of the forest sing for joy, Before Jehovah, for he cometh; for he cometh to judge the earth: he will judge the world with righteousness, and the peoples in his faithfulness. (Psalms 96:11–13)

And I saw another angel flying in mid-heaven, having the everlasting glad tidings to announce to those settled on the earth, and to every nation and tribe and tongue and people, saying with a loud voice, Fear God and give him glory, for the hour of his judgment has come; and do homage to him who has made the heaven and the earth and the sea and fountains of waters. (Revelation 14:6-7)

RESURRECTION OF BELIEVERS

The resurrection of believers in Christ takes place when Lord Jesus Christ comes again. Our corruptible bodies will be changed to incorruptible bodies in the twinkling of an eye.

Apostle Paul described it in 1 Corinthians 15:51-57, where he wrote that it was a mystery in the past, but it was revealed in the dispensation of 'Grace' period. He wrote that we shall not all sleep but will be changed and in a moment, in the twinkling of an eye, at the last trump, when our corruptible bodies will put on incorruptible bodies, and rise to immortality.

The sting of death, which is sin, and the strength of sin, which is the law, puts man to death, but the death is swallowed up in victory

SANCTIFICATION

for the believers in Christ. God gives victory over death through Lord Jesus Christ.

Those who arise from the grave when Jesus comes again will look at the grave and say, "O grave where is thy victory", while those who are caught up to be with the Lord Jesus for ever and ever will say "O death, where is thy sting?" (cf. 1 Corinthians 15:55)

The strength of sin is the law, which points our guilt, but does not save us from Sin. It is only the blood of Lord Jesus Christ that we have our salvation. The blood of Jesus cleanses us from our Sin. It is only by grace through faith in Jesus that we are saved and not by any good works. Jesus forgives us of our sins and all trespasses no matter how grave they are.

When Jesus was on this earth he never saw any one die in his presence. He saw the dead and He raised them to life. Lazarus was raised to life. This is simply because Jesus is not the author of death, but of life and He gives everlasting life.

Leslie M. John   *Page 200*

SANCTIFICATION

God punished man when he transgressed God's command and from then onward the death reigned. The death reigned from Adam to Moses even when there was no written law because man was under the dispensation of Conscience.

Satan cannot take the life of anyone who is righteous before God. Satan asked permission to end the life of Job but God denied permission to Satan. However, God granted Satan the power to torment Job.

"And the LORD said unto Satan, Behold, he is in thine hand; but save his life". (Job 2:6)

As per the prophecy in Genesis 3:15, which says God has put enmity between the serpent and the woman, the serpent is given the power to bruise the heel of the seed of the woman; but then the seed of the woman is given the power to bruise the head of Satan. This prophecy is about Jesus bruising the head of Satan and, indeed, Lord Jesus Christ defeated Satan at the Cross.

SANCTIFICATION

"Wherefore, as by one man sin entered into the world, and death by sin; and so death passed upon all men, for that all have sinned: (For until the law sin was in the world: but sin is not imputed when there is no law. Nevertheless death reigned from Adam to Moses, even over them that had not sinned after the similitude of Adam's transgression, who is the figure of him that was to come. But not as the offence, so also is the free gift. For if through the offence of one many be dead, much more the grace of God, and the gift by grace, which is by one man, Jesus Christ, hath abounded unto many. And not as it was by one that sinned, so is the gift: for the judgment was by one to condemnation, but the free gift is of many offences unto justification. For if by one man's offence death reigned by one; much more they which receive abundance of grace and of the gift of righteousness shall reign in life by one, Jesus Christ.)" (Romans 5:12-17, Cf. also Romans 6:23)

Notice the phrase "nevertheless death reigned from Adam to Moses..." The death had power on man even before the written law was given. Sin entered into the world when Adam and Eve transgressed the commandment of God. However, Lord Jesus Christ, the Son of God reconciled us to the Father by becoming sacrifice on behalf of us, and dying on the cross, bearing our sin.

Satan, who is the author of sin, has the power to cause the death of a sinner. If we are without Sin, then death has no power over us; but Scripture says all have sinned and come short of the glory of God. If we say have not sinned we are liars and we make God a liar.

"for all have sinned, and come short of the glory of God" (Romans 3:23)

"If we say that we have not sinned, we make him a liar, and his word is not in us". (1 John 1:10)

When Lazarus was dead for four days Jesus saw him and said "Our friend Lazarus sleepeth..." The disciples of Jesus took his saying at face value and thought Lazarus was, indeed, sleeping.

Leslie M. John   Page 203

SANCTIFICATION

However, Jesus spoke of the death of Lazarus and said he is dead. Jesus said that He will wake him up from his sleep, indicating that He will raise Lazarus. Martha believed and said to Jesus that she knew Lazarus would rise in the resurrection at the last day. But then, Jesus said He is the resurrection. (Cf. John: 11:13, 14, 24, 25)

"Jesus said unto her, I am the resurrection, and the life: he that believeth in me, though he were dead, yet shall he live" (John 11:25)

The departure of Lazarus from this earth was painful to Mary and Martha, who were sisters of Lazarus. How comforting it is to note that Jesus shares the grief of his followers and redeems them from their grief. Jesus was their good friend and shared their grief

"Jesus wept". (John 11:35)

Jesus raised Lazarus from his death and this was after four days had lapsed after his death. Many Jews believed in Jesus and some of them left that place to tell Pharisees about the resurrection of Lazarus that they saw.

However, the resurrection of believers in Christ, when Christ comes again is different from the resurrection of Lazarus, who was raised to console Mary and Martha and this miracle was one of the many miracles that Jesus did during his public ministry on this earth.

DEATH DEFEATED

And as it is appointed unto men once to die, but after this the judgment: (Hebrews 9:27)

God can extend the life of a person on this earth at his discretion. Hezekiah's life was extended by fifteen years when he prayed; but there came a day when he died. (2 Kings 20:6, 2 Kings 20:21. Isaiah 38:5).

Lord Jesus Christ thought it not robbery to be equal with God, but He took the form of a servant and was made likeness of men. He made himself of no reputation and humbled himself and became obedient unto death, even the most wretched death on the Cross.

SANCTIFICATION

It is because Jesus, the Son of God, who was manifest in flesh, humbled Himself so much that He was exalted by God and exalted Him. Jesus was given a name that is above every name and every knee shall bow to him. The authority of Jesus is over everything in heaven, everything in earth and everything under earth (Cf. Philippians 2:6-10).

Instead of taking on him the nature of angels, Jesus took on him the form of servant in the likeness of man, of the seed of Abraham and of David, in order that he might destroy the power of death, which is the devil.

The death, which had sting to hurt men, and the sin that caused death, which reigned from Adam to Moses, and would have continued if Jesus did not die for the salvation of men, was defeated at the cross.

The devil is defeated and the power of death is destroyed, thus rendering Satan with no power over believers in Christ. In the death and resurrection of Jesus there was a way made for

SANCTIFICATION

the deliverance of them that were subject to
the fear of death in their entire lifetime.

*"Forasmuch then as the children are partakers
of flesh and blood, he also himself likewise
took part of the same; that through death he
might destroy him that had the power of
death, that is, the devil; And deliver them who
through fear of death were all their lifetime
subject to bondage. For verily he took not on
him the nature of angels; but he took on him
the seed of Abraham". (Hebrews 2:14-16)*

As Jesus had promised He laid down His life
for the sake of sinners that they may believe in
Him and be saved and He took it back in His
resurrection. In Revelation 1:18 Jesus said...

*"I am he that liveth, and was dead; and,
behold, I am alive for evermore, Amen; and
have the keys of hell and of death"*

Lord Jesus Christ holds the key to the hell and
death, and no one can put any one in hell, or
subject one to death without the permission
from Lord Jesus Christ, who holds the key to
the hell and death.

SANCTIFICATION

However, the question is whether it is God who takes the life of a person or Satan; be it of believer or unbeliever. God permits Satan to end the life of man. He does not take the life of any person. God did not create any one to die. Causing death was not His purpose but He punished mankind with death for sinning. It is by transgression of God's command that man was punished unto death.

Satan cannot end the life of a believer in Christ, and the life of a believer in Christ does not end at any time, but it continues beyond the death. The death is only a temporary transition from earthly life to eternal life for a believer in Christ, and the believer in Christ lives for ever and ever with Lord Jesus Christ.

The death is cessation of this earthly life and a fully unconscious state for an unbeliever until he is resurrected to stand, at the end of the times, for judgment, and damnation in 'lake of fire' for ever and ever.

Death of believer should not be compared with that of unbeliever to say that the death is cessation of life for all.

TRNSITION TO NEW STRUCTURE

The first evidence that the soul of a believer in Christ shall not lie dead in the grave is seen in the words of none other than our Savior Lord Jesus Christ, who said to the repentant thief that he will be with the Lord in paradise the same day.

The prophecy of crucifixion of Jesus and that he will be numbered along with two transgressors was recorded in Isaiah 53:12. Rightly so, when Jesus was crucified two thieves were also crucified on his either side. While one of the two thieves mocked Jesus, another prayed to Jesus to remember him when Jesus comes in His kingdom. The thief, who repented before the Lord, was promised that he will be with the Lord on the same day when Jesus died.

SANCTIFICATION

"And Jesus said unto him, Verily I say unto thee, To day shalt thou be with me in paradise". (Luke 23:43)

Apostle Paul wrote that when our bodies groan and are laid to be decayed in the dust, our soul will be with the Lord, and at the first resurrection we will rise to meet the Lord in the air. It is this great hope that a believer in Christ has that his soul will not perish but will be with the Lord Jesus Christ for ever and ever.

"For we know that if our earthly house of this tabernacle were dissolved, we have a building of God, an house not made with hands, eternal in the heavens" (2 Corinthians 5:1)

"We are confident, I say, and willing rather to be absent from the body, and to be present with the Lord". (2 Corinthians 5:8)

Those believers in Christ who have gone before us will rise first to be with the Lord for ever and ever, and those that are alive when the Lord shall come with a shout, with the voice of the archangel, and with the trump of God, will be caught up to meet the Lord in the air, to be with Him for ever and ever. The sinner will rise to be judged and condemned and will be cast into 'lake of fire' along with Satan and his fallen angels where there is gnashing of teeth and torment for ever and ever.

"For the Lord himself shall descend from heaven with a shout, with the voice of the archangel, and with the trump of God: and the dead in Christ shall rise first: Then we which are alive and remain shall be caught up together with them in the clouds, to meet the Lord in the air: and so shall we ever be with the Lord". (1 Thessalonians 4:16–17)

WE WILL RISE TO LIFE

We are so privileged that once we are saved after hearing the word of truth, which is the gospel of Grace, we are sealed with Holy Spirit of promise.

"In whom ye also trusted, after that ye heard the word of truth, the gospel of your salvation: in whom also after that ye believed, ye were

sealed with that holy Spirit of promise"
Ephesians 1:13

Old Testament saints prophesied about resurrection of the bodies, and they had faith that they will see God. King David, the psalmist, knew that in the grave it is not possible to give thanks to the Lord, nor is there any remembrance of God, and, therefore, he implored the LORD to return and deliver his soul. He says he is glad and rejoices in the LORD because his flesh also shall rest in hope, because the LORD will not leave his soul in hell; nor will He suffer His Holy One (Jesus Christ) to see corruption.

It was Messianic prophecy of psalmist who prophesied that the body of Lord Jesus Christ will not see corruption in the grave. The prophecy was fulfilled, when Lord Jesus Christ rose from the dead on the third day of His crucifixion. In Jesus we have hope that we will also rise from the dead and be with Him for ever and ever.

SANCTIFICATION

Job prophesied very clearly that, even though his skin is eaten by worms in the grave, yet he will see the LORD, his redeemer, when He comes again. This is the same hope we also have in Christ that we will see Him in our glorified bodies when He comes again. Our souls are instantly taken alive to a place of comfort, commonly known as "Hades".

"For I know that my redeemer liveth, and that he shall stand at the latter day upon the earth: And though after my skin worms destroy this body, yet in my flesh shall I see God" (Job 19:25-26)

(Also Cf. Psalm16:10; 17:15; 30:3; 49:15; 73:24; 89:48; John 4:14; 1 Corinthians 15:35-49; Philippians 2:13)

Looking unto Jesus the author and finisher of our faith; who for the joy that was set before him endured the cross, despising the shame, and is set down at the right hand of the throne of God. (Hebrews 12:2)

And such were some of you: but ye are washed, but ye are sanctified, but ye are

SANCTIFICATION

justified in the name of the Lord Jesus, and by the Spirit of our God. (1 Corinthians 6:11)

But we are bound to give thanks alway to God for you, brethren beloved of the Lord, because God hath from the beginning chosen you to salvation through sanctification of the Spirit and belief of the truth: (2 Thessalonians 2:13)

It is so amazing that when our Lord comes again, our bodies will rise from the dead, and will be transformed to be glorified bodies, in the twinkling of an eye with our souls in the glorified bodies. (cf. Psalms 6:3-6; Psalms 16:8-11; Matthew 28:1-20; 1 Corinthians 15:52-54). This is perfect sanctification.

CHAPTER 14
MARTHA NEEDED
SANCTIFICATION

Jesus and His disciples decided to go to Bethany, where Mary and Martha waited for Him, seeking His intervention, when their brother Lazarus was sick. Jesus knew that Lazarus was dead even before he left for Judea from the place where He was.

Just before Jesus left for Bethany from Judea, He said to His disciples, that He was glad that He was not at Bethany. He delayed in order that He may bring glory to the Father, and thereby those who watched may believe in Him. He was sure of bringing back Lazarus to life. When Jesus came into Bethany along with His disciples, it was already four days since the dead body of Lazarus was in the grave.

Thomas, who was known as Didymus, said to his fellow disciples that they all must go to Bethany along with Jesus, even if it meant death to them. It was a very firm decision and

He believed that all good things come from Jesus.

Bethany was fifteen furlongs away from Jerusalem, and many Jews came to Martha and Mary to comfort them, after the death of Lazarus. Obviously, this shows that Mary, Martha and Lazarus were very popular in Bethany, and they had very good friends, who had close fellowship with them.

MARTHA BELIEVED

When Martha heard that Jesus was coming to their home, she went out, and met Him where He was. Mary, who perhaps was disappointed at the death of her brother, sat still at home. Martha was enthusiastic, and had zeal for the Lord. Her brother's death did not prevent her from meeting Jesus. She said to Jesus that if He were present at their home, when Lazarus was sick, the latter would not have died. Her faith was great that, even in those trying circumstances, Jesus would be able to bring some good for them, by praying to God, who, as she believed, will surely answer His prayers.

SANCTIFICATION

"Then said Martha unto Jesus, Lord, if thou hadst been here, my brother had not died" (John 11:21)

Jesus assured Martha that her brother, Lazarus would rise again. However, she thought in a different way that Lazarus would arise from the death at the last day. Then, Jesus said...

"...I am the resurrection, and the life: he that believeth in me, though he were dead, yet shall he live" John 11:25

We were all dead in trespasses but He has quickened us and promised us everlasting life. Even though we walked according to the course of this world, obeying the prince of the power of the air, "fulfilling the desires of the flesh and of the mind", God in His mercy loved us, and gave salvation to us, in response to our yielding to the pleasures of our Lord Jesus Christ, and accepting Him as our Savior. (Ref. Ephesians 2:1-6)

Our eternal abode is with the Lord Jesus Christ, and He will raise us from the dead. Death for a believer is similar to sleep in the

SANCTIFICATION

Lord, and the soul of the believer will be with the Lord immediately it leaves the physical body. He who believes in Jesus will live, even though he was physically dead. Man's physical body, which is devoid of soul and spirit, is dust that returns to dust; but believers' bodies will arise one day, as glorified bodies, when Lord Jesus Christ comes again. Bible says there is no other way and those who do not believe in Him shall have their eternity spent in 'lake of fire'.

Jesus raised Lazarus from the death and, before He raised him, He asked Martha if she believed that whoever believes in Him shall never die. Jesus was not referring to physical death, but He was referring to spiritual death versus everlasting life. Martha said she believed that Jesus was the Christ, the Son of God, who was to come into the world as prophesied in the Old Testament Scriptures.

It is time for those, who have not believed in Jesus, to take time to repent, and turn to Lord Jesus Christ. Believe Jesus is the Lord, and that He was raised from the dead. Death has no victory over a believer in Christ.

MARTHA STUMBLES

In the presence of Martha, Mary, and the Jews, who were weeping and comforting the bereaved family, Jesus commanded to remove the stone, which was laid over the cave, where the dead body of Lazarus was laid to rest for four days then.

Martha looked at Lord Jesus and said to Him "Lord, by this time he stinketh: for he hath been [dead] four days".

This was the same Martha, who said to Jesus earlier that she believed in Christ that He was the Son of God, who was to come into the world, as prophesied in the Old Testament. This was the same Martha, who said to Jesus that He was the resurrection and life, and later ran to her home to tell Mary that the Lord was coming to Bethany.

Now, when Jesus commanded that the stone covering the grave of Lazarus be removed she

SANCTIFICATION

says "Lord, by this time he stinketh: for he hath been [dead] four days". Speaking about man, his length of days on this earth, and his riches, Psalmist says:

"Behold, thou hast made my days [as] an handbreadth; and mine age [is] as nothing before thee: verily every man at his best state [is] altogether vanity. Selah" Psalm 39:5

If only God were to punish us according to the measure of our sins, we would not have deserved forgiveness or be able to stand before God. However,

"...God so loved the world, that he gave his only begotten Son, that whosoever believeth in him should not perish, but have everlasting life." John 3:16

Lord Jesus Christ paid price for our sins, made us righteous and justified. There is no condemnation to those who believe in Him.

Jesus admonishes Martha reminding her that if she believed in Him she will see the glory of God. Then, they took away the stone from the place where Lazarus was laid to rest. Then Jesus lifted up His eyes and prayed to the Father. In His prayer Jesus thanked the Father for hearing His prayer and said that the Father always hears Him. He prayed so in order that those who stood by Him may believe that the Father sent Him.

Jesus, after praying, cried out with a loud voice "Lazarus come forth". Notice Jesus called the dead man by his name; else, perhaps many dead would have come forth. The voice of Jesus was so powerful that the dead Lazarus rose to life and came forth. Another very noticeable fact is that the hand and foot of Lazarus were still bound with grave-clothes, and his face was bound with a napkin.

Comparison with the rising of the Lord Jesus Christ Himself, much later, when His hour was come, would show that the napkin that was bound on the face of Jesus was laid aside nicely folded, indicating that He Himself unloosened His bindings, and then folded the napkin that was bound on his head, and placed it at the side where His head was laid.

SANCTIFICATION

There was no assistance required for unloosening the wrap around the dead body of Jesus in the tomb. The tomb was covered with a stone, which was sealed and Jews made sure that no one stole His body. There was no scope of spreading false rumors that He was not raised from the dead, and yet there are many, in some circles, in the present generation, spreading false rumors that He did not die on the cross, nor did He rise from the dead. Indeed, Jesus died according to Scriptures, and there is evidence secular history as well. He appeared before many men, at different intervals, for forty days after His resurrection and before His ascension into heaven. He showed nail marks on his hands and feet to Thomas. He was the first-fruits.

Lord Jesus Christ commanded that Lazarus be unbound of the grave-clothes and the napkin that he may go. Thus, Lazarus was raised to life only to die again later because he was mortal, but Lord Jesus Christ was the Son of God, in the form of man, and therefore, His body did not see corruption in the grave and He rose in glorified body, which could pass closed doors, eat fish, appear and disappear at His will instantly at desired place.

It is the blessed hope of all believers in Christ that the dead will rise and receive glorified bodies, instantly, and those who are alive will follow them in similar glorified bodies, transformed at the twinkling of an eye, when they are 'caught up' at the coming of Lord Jesus again. (Cf. 1 Thessalonians 4:16–17, and 1 Corinthians 15:52)

MARTHA SERVES FOOD

Jesus went to Bethany six days before the Passover and was entreated well at the house of Lazarus, whom He raised from the dead. At the supper table, one among many who were seated was Lazarus along with Jesus and Martha served the Lord.

MARY SERVES THE LORD

While Martha was serving at the table, Mary anointed the feet of Jesus with a pound of ointment of spikenard, which was very expensive, and wiped His feet with her hair.

SANCTIFICATION

The house was filled with the ointment that was highly fragrant, and Judas Iscariot, one of the disciples of Jesus, who later betrayed Him, questioned to Mary, as to why she wasted so much money to buy the ointment and pour it on the feet of Jesus.

Judas Iscariot, a hypocrite, and a cunning man, who hankered after money, questioned Mary not because he really cared for the poor, but because he was treasurer, a thief who kept the bag, wherein money was cast into, as offerings. Then Lord Jesus instructed Judas Iscariot and others in the home to let Mary alone without troubling her mind, and allow her to worship Him as she preferred.

Many Jews who were present in Lazarus home were there to see him alive. They were there not only to see Jesus but to see Lazarus, whom He raised from the dead. Chief priests conspired to kill Lazarus because by the resurrection of Lazarus many Jews believed in Jesus.

MARTHA COMPAINS

Martha complained to Jesus when she felt that she was overburdened serving at the tables, while Mary was at the feet of Jesus wiping His feet with her hair after pouring the ointment of spikenard on His feet. She prayed to Jesus to let Mary to help her in serving at the tables, but Jesus said Mary has chosen the good part of the whole service, and therefore, she will not be let go from serving Him.

Although Martha did not lose salvation, she lost some blessings firstly for doubting Jesus and His power, and secondly complaining to Jesus about her sister Mary, and thirdly by her choice she chose serving food to the guests than the Son of God, who was in the form of man. Martha chose a very good part of entertaining the guests; however, Mary chose to give pre-eminence to the Lord. Martha needed a small reproof from the Lord to set her for the service of the Lord in preference to the service of the earthly benefits (cf. John 12:1-11 and Luke 10:38-42)

THE LORD ANWERS

And Jesus answered and said unto her, Martha, Martha, thou art careful and troubled about many things: But one thing is needful: and Mary hath chosen that good part, which shall not be taken away from her. (Luke 10:41–42)

CHAPTER 15
I WILL EXTOL THEE

"I will extol thee, my God, O king; and I will bless thy name for ever and ever" (Psalms 145:1)

Saul was king over Israel, but he failed to obey the commandment of the LORD fully. David fulfilled the desires of the LORD, and had great zeal for Him. David sings song to the Lord God, who forgave his sins, even that of his adultery with Bathsheba, and conspiring against her husband Uriah, because the LORD is forgiving, gracious and full of compassion. David fulfilled the desires of the LORD. The Lord "...slow to anger and of great mercy".

David was a man of wars and he was triumphant in all his battles, where he sought the LORD's permission before he went for war, but on one occasion he was defeated because he numbered his army, which displeased the LORD.

SANCTIFICATION

David eulogized the LORD for his mercy towards him and sang high praises to the LORD. He was all praise to God singing blessings to His name promising that he would sing for ever and ever; everyday.

Truly, God is great, and deserves all our praises and his greatness is unsearchable. His creation displays His glory, and yet there are some who demand proof of his existence. The beauty of butterfly, the Sun, the Moon, the Stars, the starfish, the tiny birds, the whale, the beautiful flowers, display His beauty, might, and glory. He is the LORD of all.

One generation shall praise and declare His works to another and men speak of awesome acts. As David declares His greatness, we do too. We all sing and His great goodness in memory of the sacrifice of Lord Jesus Christ and His crucifixion in order that we may not perish but have everlasting life.

"The LORD is good to all: and his tender mercies are over all his works". Psalm 145:9

Leslie M. John   *Page 228*

SANCTIFICATION

The LORD, Jehovah is His name, and every work of Him shall praise Him and His saints bless Him, and exalt His name above all other names. Every generation will speak of the glory of His kingdom and talk of His power. They will make known, to the subsequent generations, His mighty works. The LORD sent tokens and wonders into the midst of Egyptians and upon Pharaoh; He slew mighty kings such as Sihon, king of the Amorites, and Og, king of Bashan, and all the kingdoms of Canaan. (cf. Psalm 135:9-11)

The LORD's kingdom is everlasting kingdom and His dominion endures throughout all generations. He upholds all that fall and praise Him. He raises them if they bow down to Him. Salvation belongs to Him and to Him alone. He is the King of kings; He is the LORD of lords.

The eyes of the LORD run to and fro throughout the whole earth in search of those whose eyes wait upon Him and He gives food, clothing and shelter to them in due season. He shows that He is strong on behalf of them whose heart is perfect toward him. David was

SANCTIFICATION

surely an example to look at as to how his heart was perfect toward the LORD, but here is a case of Asa, who was Rehoboam's grandson. Rehoboam was grandson of David. When Asa did right in the sight of the LORD the land was quite for ten years.

Obed, the prophet spoke to Asa and said to him, to entire tribe of Judah, and of Benjamin that the Lord was with them, and if they seek they will find Him, but if they forsake Him, He will forsake them. It was time when for a long time they did not have a true God, and a teaching prophet, and Law. However, when they turned to the LORD God of Israel, and sought Him, they found Him. Even in the prevailing times of turmoil, great vexations, when nations destroyed nations, and cities destroyed cities, Asa and His people had rest in the LORD. The LORD said to them:

"Be ye strong therefore, and let not your hands be weak: for your work shall be rewarded" (2 Chronicles 15:7)

SANCTIFICATION

Asa heard words of courage from the LORD, conveyed through the prophet Obed, he became courageous and put away all the abominable idols out of the land of Judah and Benjamin, and also from the cities which he conquered from mount Ephraim.

Asa honored the LORD by renewing the altar of the LORD, which was before the porch of the LORD. When the people saw that the LORD was with Asa, they fell in obeisance to him. The people were from the "House of Judah", and strangers from Ephraim, and Manasseh, and out of Simeon. In the third month of the fifteenth year of Asa's reign they offered to the LORD the spoil which they brought from those cities. They entered into a covenant with God that they will seek the true God Jehovah, the God of Israel with all their heart and with all their soul. They made a strong covenant and swore to the LORD that those who do not seek the LORD, the God of Israel, will be put to death. Therefore, the LORD gave them perfect rest.

SANCTIFICATION

Asa did not hesitate to remove his own mother, Maachah, from being queen, because she made an idol in a grove. "Asa cut down her idol, and stamped it, and burnt it at the brook Kidron." However, he did not remove high places away out of Israel; nevertheless, he was perfect all his days. Therefore, there was no war until the thirty fifth year of his reign. (Cf. 2 Chronicles 15:1-19)

As Asa entered into thirty sixth year of his reign, he wandered away from God, and stole silver and gold from the house of the LORD, and sent them to Benhadad, king of Syria, who was living in Damascus, seeking a league between them. Asa told a lie that their fathers had a league that Benhadad should break his league Baasha, the King of Israel. Benhadad agreed and took silver and gold, which was stolen by Asa, from the house of the LORD. Thereafter, Benhadad attacked Baasha, king of Israel and smote him and Ijon, Dan, Abelmaim, and all the store cities of Naphtali.

Baasha, King of Israel, who was building a fortified city, called Ramah, in order to see that the trade between the "House of Israel" and the "House of Judah" might stop. It may be recalled here that because King Solomon's disobedience, his kingdom (of whole of Israel) was divided into two. The northern kingdom was known as the "House of Israel" and the southern kingdom was known as the "House of Judah". As Benhadad made very intelligent move of attacking Baasha from northern side, while his men were building Ramah at the borders of Judah, he successfully humiliated Baasha.

The peace that Asa had for twenty five years after he and his men made a forceful covenant with the LORD was utterly lost, when he chose to steal from the house of the LORD, silver and gold, to connive with alien king, Benhadad, the king of Syria. Benhadad, king of Syria destroyed the cities of, Baasha, the king of Israel.

The LORD God was very angry and He sent His word through Prophet Hanani to him that Asa will have henceforth wars in his kingdom and will not have rest. The result of the "House of

Judah" fighting with the "House of Israel" resulted in alien king to benefit and escape with his host.

Asa did not rely on the LORD, but relied upon the king of Syria, and eventually the host of the king of Syria escaped out of his hand. If God could give Ethiopians and Lubims, a huge host, who had many chariots and horsemen, (which was erstwhile strength of the army), into the hands of Asa when he relied on the LORD, then He could have delivered king of Syria, as well, into his hands, but the LORD did not give victory to Asa, because the latter did not rely upon the LORD God of Israel.

"And at that time Hanani the seer came to Asa king of Judah, and said unto him, Because thou hast relied on the king of Syria, and not relied on the LORD thy God, therefore is the host of the king of Syria escaped out of thine hand. Were not the Ethiopians and the Lubims a huge host, with very many chariots and horsemen? yet, because thou didst rely on the LORD, he delivered them into thine hand. For the eyes of the LORD run to and fro

SANCTIFICATION

throughout the whole earth, to shew himself strong in the behalf of them whose heart is perfect toward him. Herein thou hast done foolishly: therefore from henceforth thou shalt have wars". (2 Chronicles 16:7–9)

The LORD is near to all those who call on Him in truth. He fulfills the desires of them that fear Him and hears their cry and saves them. The LORD preserves all those who love Him; but He will destroy all the wicked.

We sing to the Lord Jesus Christ just as David sang to the LORD God.

"My mouth shall speak the praise of the LORD: and let all flesh bless his holy name for ever and ever" Psalm 145:21

SANCTIFICATION